Teaching Kids to Care and Share

Teaching Kids to Care & Share

300+ Mission & Service Ideas for Children

Jolene L. Roehlkepartain

Abingdon Press
Nashville

TEACHING KIDS TO CARE AND SHARE:
300+ MISSION AND SERVICE IDEAS FOR CHILDREN

Copyright © 2000 by Abingdon Press

This book is printed on recycled, acid-free, elemental-chlorine–free paper.

Library of Congress Cataloging-in-Publication Data

Roehlkepartain, Jolene L., 1962–
    Teaching kids to care & share: 300+ mission & service ideas for children / Jolene L. Roehlkepartain.
        p. cm.
    Includes bibliographical references and index.
    ISBN 0-687-08428-8 (alk. paper)
     1. Caring—Religious aspects—Christianity—Study and teaching—Activity programs.   2. Sharing—Religious aspects—Christianity—Study and teaching—Activity programs.   3. Christian education of children.   4. Church work with children. I. Title: Teaching kids to care and share.   II. Title.

    BV4647.S9 R64 2000
    268'.432—dc21

                                                                                                99-055636

Scripture quotations noted TEV are from Today's English Version—Second Edition. Copyright © 1992 by American Bible Society. Used by permission.

Scripture quotations noted NIV are taken from the Holy Bible: New International Version. Copyright © 1973, 1978, 1984 by the International Bible Society. Used by permission of Zondervan Publishing House. All rights reserved.

00 01 02 03 04 05 06 07 08 09—10 9 8 7 6 5 4 3 2 1

MANUFACTURED IN THE UNITED STATES OF AMERICA

To Franc and Edna Wagschal
who model, teach, and live rich lives full of service and mission

Contents

Part 1

The Beginnings of Mission & Service

"There is a call to us, a call of service—that we join with others to try to make things better in this world," said Dorothy Day, cofounder of a religious movement in the 1930s that promoted service, peace, and social change.[1] That call is for all people, of all ages, including children.

The spirit of service in individuals is born early on. Infants have an innate response of crying when others around them are upset. Toddlers often offer a toy or a hug to another distressed toddler. Preschool children enthusiastically volunteer to help. Elementary-age children often come up with ideas to make life better for people in hard times. As children grow, their spirit of service will grow—as long as we nurture that spirit.

When you ask service-minded teenagers when they first volunteered, most of them say they started by age fourteen, with 49 percent starting before or by age twelve.[2] "These findings suggest that volunteering is an activity most likely to be cultivated in childhood and during the early teenage years," says the Independent Sector in its national survey *Volunteering and Giving*.[3] If we want to instill a sense of service and mission in young people, we need to start when they're young. And we need to keep giving them new opportunities to serve year after year so that service becomes a part of who they are.

Church is the number one place where young people learn about service and volunteer activities, say researchers at the Independent Sector. Sixty-eight percent say they find out about service projects through church, whereas 28 percent learn about these activities through school, which ranks second.[4] Congregations are a critical place for children to learn about caring and sharing.

The Biblical Basis for Mission and Service

The concepts of caring and sharing are also central themes throughout scripture. The Bible is full of passages about caring for people who are poor or oppressed. Deuteronomy 10:18-19 commands us to love and care for others, just as 2 Corinthians 9 compares service and mission to planting seeds. "Remember that the person who plants few seeds will have a small crop; the one who plants many seeds will have a large crop. You should each give, then, as you have decided, not with regret or out of a sense of duty; for God loves the one who gives gladly" (2 Corinthians 9:6-7 TEV).

Christians get involved in mission and service for different reasons. Some cite justice issues, taking seriously the message in Micah 6:8 "to do what is just, to show constant love, and to live in humble fellowship with our God" (TEV). Others point to the messages of Jesus in Luke 12:32-34 and Luke 4. "The Spirit of the Lord is upon me, because he has chosen me to bring good news to the poor. He has sent me to proclaim liberty to the captives and recovery of sight to the blind, to set free the oppressed and announce that the time has come when the Lord will save his people" (Luke 4:18-19 TEV). Serving others was also a major message in Paul's ministry, as described in Romans 15:25-27.

Throughout the Bible, stories and passages emphasize service and mission as fundamentals of faith. When we familiarize children with these scriptures while also engaging them in hands-on service and mission projects, we ground them in faith.

The Basics of Doing Mission and Service with Children

Children get more out of mission and service projects when we gear these activities to their age and understanding. Too often, it's easy to create projects that are either too complex or too simple. That's why the more than 325 ideas in this book are designed for three different age groups of children: for three- to five-year-olds, for six- to nine-year-olds, and for ten- to twelve-year-olds. Creating a service project for a four-year-old is different from designing one for an eleven-year-old.

● **Working with 3- to 5-year-olds**—Children at this age can easily pick up on other's feelings, and they are learning to identify broad emotions, such as happiness, anger, and sadness. By labeling emotions so children recognize them while also learning helping behaviors, we can instill a sense of service in children. When a preschooler offers a crayon to a crying preschooler with a broken crayon, this is a form of service. It may be a simple act of service, but it's a critical act for this age group. Put these simple acts together, and you lay the foundational work for lifelong service.

Sharing is a hard concept for preschoolers. When things are taken away, children can't comprehend the idea that they'll ever get the items back. Emphasizing the concept of sharing over and over is another crucial way to instill a sense of service in young children. When we let children take turns and give them simple opportunities to help, we are giving them ways to serve.

Creating hands-on, tangible projects for this age group cements the value of service and mission in children's heads. "Young children are developmentally concrete," says Ann Shoemaker in *Teaching Young Children Through Service.* "The younger the child involved in service-learning, the closer at hand the recipient of your service should be."[5] Concrete projects such as visiting people in a nursing home and bringing a snack to people building a Habitat house make a strong impression on young children.

● **Working with 6- to 9-year-olds**—While preschoolers tend to be possessive about *things*, children at this age tend to be possessive about *people*. They have difficulty sharing friends and can easily feel rejected. Teaching children that people can have more than one friend and that people can work together is part of what service projects can provide.

True empathy, the ability to put yourself in another person's place, starts to develop in a child between the ages of six and eight. Mission and service projects can emphasize this growing awareness of empathy. Children can learn about the restraints of having to go through the day in a wheelchair or about not having enough money to buy food. Although children are still apt to see the world from their point of view, service and mission projects can help expand their view so they can begin to see the world from other people's perspectives.

● **Working with 10- to 12-year-olds**—By this age, children have developed a number of skills and capacities to contribute more to mission and service projects. They also now know that empathy and self-assertiveness can coexist. When adults help children see how they can serve others and take care of themselves at the same time, children learn how not to burn out and be self-sacrificing.

Children at this age also enjoy having discussions about service in addition to doing the work of service. Include more in-depth Bible studies and discussion times with service projects to give children the chance to ask questions and puzzle over situations they see and experience.

Adults can really capitalize on this age group's willingness and openness to do mission and service projects. "They like to try new things; like to see what they can accomplish," say the authors of *Your Ten- to Fourteen-Year-Old.*[6] Although children at this age can have stubborn streaks, they often can contribute a lot—and enthusiastically—when given projects that interest and challenge them.

● **Working with children who have disabilities**—All children can serve, and all children benefit from doing service projects. Sometimes it can be challenging to create service projects that are inclusive for children who have disabilities, but it's an important challenge to take up. If you have children with attention-deficit and hyperactivity, create short, well-structured projects. Children with physical disabilities can participate more easily if you bring the project to them. Children with learning disabilities feel more included when reflection activities after a service project are done as verbal discussions instead of pen-and-paper activities. In the book *An Asset-Builder's Guide to Service-Learning,* you'll find a chapter on how to make service projects work for a wide diversity of children, and the chapter also includes a sidebar titled "Service-Learning Project Possibilities for Students with Disabilities."[7]

- **Working with children who seem to have few resources**—It's often uncomfortable asking children to give or serve, particularly if one or more of the children seems more like an ideal recipient. But what a child has isn't the point. Luke 21:1-4 emphasizes the responsibility of giving for *everyone*. "Jesus looked around and saw rich people dropping their gifts in the Temple treasury, and he also saw a very poor widow dropping in two little copper coins. He said, 'I tell you that this poor widow put in more than all the others. For the others offered their gifts from what they had to spare of their riches; but she, poor as she is, gave all she had to live on'" (TEV).

Seven Keys of Meaningful Mission and Service

While understanding children is a key to a successful service or mission project, there are other keys that are just as important. These include:

- **Key #1: Make projects concrete**—Children learn best by using their senses. Using a hammer, picking up trash, visiting the sick, collecting canned food, playing board games with residents of a nursing home—these are concrete experiences that children can easily relate to and ones that get them excited.

- **Key #2: Work with existing networks**—Creating a mission or service project can be a lot of work. There's no sense in reinventing something that already exists. Contact your regional denominational office, your local community volunteer organization, or specific organizations (such as Habitat for Humanity or a food bank or shelf) and plug into their existing structures. Most of these places are looking for volunteers, and most would be happy to work with you.

- **Key #3: Empower children**—Create projects that are meaningful, not ones that just keep children busy. Empower children by having them plan, suggest ideas, and take ownership so they feel like essential contributors. While younger children (ages three to five) don't have the planning skills that older children do (those ages ten to twelve), preschool children can vote between two or three service projects that adults suggest.

- **Key #4: Debrief children about experiences afterward**—No two service or mission projects are alike. An activity can trigger different feelings and opinions in children. That's why it's important to have time to ask children about their experience after the project. Find out what they liked about it, what they didn't like (children can get turned off if they feel bored, too hungry, overheated, or if they detect that they were in the way), and what they learned. Even difficult experiences can have teachable moments. For example, children can become upset when they're painting a fence for a homebound person who spends her or his time criticizing their work and warning them not to step on the flowers. Learning that we should help all people—even the ones who are grouchy—is an important lesson.

- **Key #5: Line up your resources**—Disorganization can quickly kill children's enthusiasm for a mission or service project. Make sure you have all the needed supplies ready before the project begins. Be prepared by gathering the snacks you need. Make a first-aid kit available. Also ensure that you have enough adult volunteers to assist with the project. Be clear about each person's role and the expectations you have.

- **Key #6: Dovetail the project with your church's mission**—Get a copy of your church's mission statement and refer to it each time you're choosing a mission or service project. Encourage support for your service projects from key congregational leaders by keeping church staff and lay leaders informed about the projects your children are doing. Show these leaders how your projects enhance your congregation's mission.

- **Key #7: Have fun**—An essential ingredient of a successful mission or service project for children is fun. Play some games during the activity to help break up the intensity and seriousness of the project. Have snacks. Sing songs. Plan some enjoyable activities you can do together as a group for those times when children begin to tire and need a break. While it's true that you want to get something accomplished, you also want to instill a lifelong interest in mission and service. Having fun helps.

The Hope of Mission and Service

While mission and service can instill hope in the people who are served, acts of service can also raise the spirits and hopes of the children who participate in these projects. While it's rare to have a single life-changing service project, there are moments that arise that give children a strong sense of satisfaction and enthusiasm. When goals are surpassed and recipients give hugs, children feel good about what they're doing.

We can also bring hope by creating ways for families to serve together. Many families are interested in doing mission and service projects together, although they rarely have opportunities to do so. Once, twice, or three times a year, create a congregation-wide family project that has activities for people of all ages. This could include serving a meal at a soup kitchen (even parents with infants and toddlers can have a meaningful role in mingling with the guests and getting to know them), assisting a food bank in sorting donations, or doing a fix-up project (either at the church or at someone's home). Besides giving opportunities for families to serve, these projects can also help them feel more connected to your church and to other families since service projects have a community-building nature.

Hope is one of the best gifts that a mission and service project can bring. These projects give recipients hope for a better day, a better future, a better life. And helping gives children hope that the small things they do really make a difference. That's because they see that hope become real. When a child who is hospitalized squeals at receiving a teddy bear, the children present see that hope is alive and that hope is something they *can* give.

Part 2

The Actions of Mission & Service

From creating dessert cookbooks to having baby-food drives, you'll find more than 325 service and mission ideas in this section. Each of the thirty-five action topics listed alphabetically (from Advocate to Write) include at least three ideas for three- to five-year-olds, three ideas for six- to nine-year-olds, and three ideas for ten- to twelve-year-olds. Some topics, such as Care For, Collect, Heal, Read, and Repair also include additional ideas that children of all ages can do.

These ideas are meant to be just that: *beginning ideas*. Use them. Change them. Adapt them. Add to them. Maybe you like the idea but want to change the intended audience. Go ahead and do that. Maybe you like doing something for the intended audience, but the idea just doesn't quite work; so do something different instead. These ideas are meant to get your own creative juices flowing so that when you think of doing service projects with children you don't just collect canned food and wash cars. You'll do something creative and something that fits the developmental abilities of the children you're working with.

So jump in. Find some service and mission ideas that pique your interest and get started. The people you serve will thank you. And so will the children doing the work. Service is something that benefits everyone— the givers and the receivers.

• Advocate •

Throughout our communities, our country, our world, we need to advocate for others. There are countless people who are poor or oppressed, people who have insurmountable difficulties, people who need others to advocate and stand up for them.

"Justice will be the measuring line for the foundation, and honesty will be its plumb line," says Isaiah 28:17*a* (TEV). For some people, advocacy is about justice. For others it's about mercy. What's important is not the driving force behind the advocacy but the steps taken to "do what is just, to show constant love, and to live in humble fellowship with our God" (Micah 6:8*b* TEV).

Ideas for 3- to 5-Year-olds

- **Encourage preschoolers to share a piece of candy from their Halloween trick-or-treating or their Easter baskets for a congregation-wide candy drive.** Discuss how homeless children may not get candy on holidays and how everyone can give a little to make a big difference for these children. When you finish the drive, invite the children to go with you to give the candy to a homeless shelter.

- **Be alert to situations in your community that encourage advocacy.** For example, a storm can knock out power and damage trees. Flooding can occur. Maybe a terrible accident resulted in a lot of people getting hurt. Use these situations to create mission and service projects. For example, preschoolers can donate stuffed animals to children who lost their toys in a flood or tornado.

- **Talk about Jeremiah 21:12, emphasizing how helping others is something we should do *every day*.** Have children crouch on the floor and jump up and say "every day" before crouching back down again when you name things they should do every day, such as get dressed in the morning, do what parents say, brush teeth, be nice, eat lunch, clean up, and help others.

Ideas for 6- to 9-Year-olds

- **Organize a baby blanket drive.** Contact a local hospital, low-income child-care center, police station, or child protection agency to see who would benefit most from a baby blanket drive.

- **Read aloud Amos 5:24:** "Let justice flow like a stream, and righteousness like a river that never goes dry" (TEV). Discuss how we can never check off our lists advocating for those who are poor or those who need our help. As a group, ask children to name things that are unfair, such as children bullying other children and people who are favored over others. Talk about the simple things children can do to stand up for others, such as befriending them, telling adults when situations get out of hand, and using their words instead of their fists.

- **Advocate for animals who need help.** After getting permission from parents and the shelter, take children to an animal shelter. Children can help clean up, play with animals, put fresh water in water bowls, and do other things (things that the animal shelter deems good ideas) to make the temporary home a better place for animals.

Ideas for 10- to 12-Year-olds

- **Have children memorize Micah 3:8:** "But as for me, the LORD fills me with his spirit and power, and gives me a sense of justice and . . . courage" (TEV). As a group, talk about the importance of courage in doing advocacy work. Study one of the important advocates of history, such as Martin Luther King Jr., Mother Teresa, Gandhi, or Cesar Chavez. Examine how the person's religious beliefs impacted her or his advocacy work.

- **Ask children to write letters to their congresspersons about an issue they care about deeply.** To find out about current legislation before the House and the Senate, call (202) 225-1772, or read the political portion of your local newspaper. Children can write to senators at: The United States Senate, Washington, DC 20510, and to representatives at: The United States House of Representatives, Washington, DC 20515. You also can do this with your state and community legislature.

- **With the children's help, identify an area of your church that needs attention.** For example, maybe there's a room that no one uses because it's filled with stuff. Perhaps there's a portion of the church grounds that is full of weeds and hard to care for because of a tangle of bushes or trees. Or maybe there's a bathroom that gets dirty really fast. Have children survey church members to find out their opinions of the situation and what should be done about it. Then have your young people create some solutions that they can put into practice and present them to your church's governing board.

Helpful organizations

For the address, phone number, and web site of these organizations, see the Mission and Service Index starting on page 119.

- **Church World Service**—Advocate for refugees, people who are hungry, and those living in difficult situations through this religious organization.

- **Disability Rights Education and Defense Fund Inc.**—Use information from this organization to help advocate for people who live with physical impairments.

· Befriend ·

The Great Commandment in Matthew 22:37-40 is clear. Not only should we love God but we should also love our neighbors as ourselves. That means all neighbors, the ones we like and the ones we wish would move away. Jesus also makes it clear in Matthew 5:43-48 that we are to love our enemies and to pray for them. Throughout the gospel, the message of caring and befriending others is strong.

Unfortunately, few service projects give children the chance to interact and befriend other people. It's easier to organize car washes and canned food drives. Creating service projects that emphasize interaction can be more difficult and more tricky to measure in terms of success. It's easier to count three hundred cans at the end of a food drive than it is to see whether any difference results from providing opportunities for children to hang out with adults or other children. Yet these relationships are essential to the Christian faith—and to service.

Ideas for 3- to 5-Year-olds

● **Arrange to have someone in your church take a class picture when you know most children will be present.** (These typically work best one of the first two Sundays of the school year.) Make a copy for each child along with a list that identifies the name of each child. Hang an enlargement of the picture in your classroom along with the list of names. This helps children learn one another's names and also feel like part of the group.

● **Teach preschoolers the central message of 1 John 4:7-8:** "Love one another" (TEV). Every time you gather as a group, do at least one community-building activity that encourages children to learn one another's names and to build relationships. For example, at the beginning of your time together, have the children sit in a circle and say their name and their favorite from a topic that you choose. (Stimulating topics include favorite colors, pets, food, animals, restaurants, toys, etc.)

● **Always be on the lookout for teachable moments about *befriending*.** For example, sometimes you might find an injured bird or cat when you go for a walk. As a group you can befriend the hurt animal and make sure it gets proper care. Be cautious when approaching injured animals, however. Claws, beaks, and teeth can transmit disease as well as scratch and cut. Or if a new child joins your class during the middle of the school year, be intentional about reaching out to help the child feel included.

Ideas for 6- to 9-Year-olds

● **As a group, talk about different situations in which someone seems left out.** (For example, a child who eats alone at the school cafeteria, a neighbor who lives alone, a homeless person who hangs out

Teaching Kids to Care & Share

near your church.) Encourage children to notice these people and to reach out to children (and to adults only when accompanied by an adult they know) to help people feel included. For example, a child can sit by a new child at school and play with that child to help that child feel included. A child can team up with a parent to visit a neighbor who lives alone, just to say hello.

● **Read 1 Peter 4:8-9 aloud.** Talk about how it's important to love each other and to be giving in our love. Find out if there's a child (or an adult) in your church who has a chronic illness. Visit and befriend that person. Arrange to play games with the person, bring occasional treats, send cards, and make phone calls. Make opportunities for relationships to be built.

● **Give children a homework assignment of either calling or visiting someone in their extended family.** Encourage children to ask questions to find out more about the person and to recount their experience the next time you get together. Talk about how befriending other people requires that we take the initiative and contact people. We shouldn't wait for others to contact us.

Ideas for 10- to 12-Year-olds

● **Ask the group to study Romans 12:9-13.** Have the children write sentences on construction paper about what this scripture suggests they do as God's servants. Have children create a "Being in God's Service" display for your church with these construction-paper sentences. Display these important sentences on a bulletin board or wall (get permission first).

● **Together, brainstorm ideas on how your group can befriend the earth in a way that's meaningful and exciting.** (Children often are bored by litter pick-ups by this age.) Maybe they will want to learn more about a polluted stream in your community and figure out ways to purify it. Or they may want to plant flowers in an overgrown garden bed at your church. If children have difficulty coming up with ideas, take a walking tour of your church grounds or neighborhood for ideas.

● **Partner with another class of children who are the same age in a different congregation.** For example, if you're an urban church, team up with a suburban congregation. Or if your church is predominantly white, team up with a more ethnically diverse group. Arrange for visits twice a year (once to your congregation and once to the other congregation) and create community-building activities to encourage relationships to form. Try to do this over a two- or three-year period since it takes awhile to build relationships.

Helpful organizations

For the address, phone number, and web site of these organizations, see the Mission and Service Index starting on page 119.

● **Friends of the Earth**—This organization provides information on ways to improve the environment.

● **Generations United**—Part of the Child Welfare League, this program promotes intergenerational understanding and interaction.

• Care For •

Three times Jesus asked Peter, "Do you love me?" in John 21:15-17. Each time Peter replied that he did. Jesus said—all three times—to "take care of my sheep" (TEV). The image of the shepherd caring for the sheep is pervasive throughout scripture. It's an important message that we should follow today: a message that we should care—and act on that caring.

There are countless ways for children to care for others, whether that be for other people, for animals, for the environment, or for important causes. Caring is one of the most fundamental ways to serve.

Ideas for All Children

• **Create birthday buddies with members of your congregation.** Find out the month and dates of the birthdays of all the children and adults in your congregation. Offer a churchwide function or gathering so that children and adults can get together according to the month in which they were born. Provide a list of questions for people to talk about, such as: What was your favorite birthday? Why? What do you like doing best on your birthday? What's your favorite birthday treat? What age do you think is best? Why? Creating a caring congregation requires finding ways to get people who typically may not interact talking to each other. The use of birthday buddies is another way to form these connections.

• **Create a "Prayer Care Line" for children to discuss what they're concerned about and want the group to pray about.** Children may be reluctant to share at first, so have other concerns you can start with, such as mentioning a congregational member who is sick, or about the weather (particularly if there have been a lot of storms), or your feelings about someone or something (such as feeling glad that you just got a new puppy). Each week, invite children to participate (but don't force them) and watch what gradually unfolds. Explain that praying is another way of caring.

Ideas for 3- to 5-Year-olds

● **Invite children to each bring a teddy bear (have extras available for those who might forget), or give each child a teddy bear sticker to wear.** Play "Care Bears" by having children sit in a circle with one child sitting in the middle of the circle. Go around the circle and have each child name one thing he or she likes about the person in the middle. (Holding a teddy bear often helps a child feel less self-conscious and more secure.) When everyone has said something, have the child in the middle join the rest of the circle while another child takes the middle. Do this until everyone has had a chance to be in the middle. Afterward talk about how the words we say to people show how we care about them.

● **Talk about Genesis 2:15 and how God placed people in the Garden of Eden to take care of it.** Discuss the different places that preschoolers have to care for. At home, they care for their rooms. At church, they care for their classroom. If they attend a preschool or child-care center during the week, they care for the spaces they are in there. Brainstorm with the children about the different ways they can care for these living spaces (such as picking things up off the floor, straightening items on the shelf, putting away toys, emptying the garbage, etc.). Create a pocket planner from the ideas children come up with to care for their church. Make this pocket planner out of a piece of posterboard and tape on pockets made out of large index cards. Use smaller index cards to write the names of children—one on each card. On each pocket, draw a picture of a caring action, such as turning off the lights when you leave the room, getting a book for reading time, throwing away napkins after a snack, and putting away toys. Place one child's name in each pocket listing an activity. Each week, change the names around so children do different activities.

• **Have a classroom pet(s), such as goldfish in an aquarium or a bowl, gerbils, hamsters, or guinea pigs.** Pets are a great way to teach preschoolers how to care. If having a classroom pet seems like too much work, ask someone to periodically bring a pet to visit your class. Dogs and cats are often big hits, and children can learn how to pet them carefully and interact with animals in caring ways. For example, you could create "circle friends" where children form a circle around a visiting pet and owner who sit in the middle. This way the pet can be more easily supervised as it roams around the circle and be less overwhelmed if you allow children to touch the animal only when the pet approaches them.

Ideas for 6- to 9-Year-olds

• **Read aloud the parable of the good Samaritan in Luke 10:25-37.** Emphasize that verse 34 tells the story of how the good Samaritan cared for the injured man. After studying the story closely together, make a class list of all the different ways the good Samaritan cared for the hurt man. Then make a list of the ways that children can care for their friends and family when they are sick or hurt.

• **Make simple get-well cards by having children place a bandage on the front of a construction-paper card and writing "Get Well Soon" on the inside.** Invite them to add more decorations if they like. Use these cards when classmates are sick or when you hear of other congregational members who are not feeling well.

• **Whenever a baby is born in your church, create a care package to welcome the newborn.** Locate a parent who has access to a school book club (generally, these groups offer books for purchase at less than two to three dollars) and buy a number of picture books that would be appropriate for your class to give. Then have the class make a card and vote on which book to give to the new baby. As a class, visit the baby (after getting permission from the parents of your children and the parents of the new baby) to present the gift.

Ideas for 10- to 12-Year-olds

• **Create Care Bags for children in hospitals and with long-term ill-**

nesses at home. Brainstorm with the children about things that they think would be good for someone who is sick. Items might include: crayons, markers, tablets of plain paper, coloring books, puzzle books, stickers, books, trading cards, etc. Use one-gallon zipper bags to hold the items. See if you can get congregational members to donate money or items for these bags.

● **Ask for a volunteer to read aloud 1 Timothy 3:5:** "For if a man does not know how to manage his own family, how can he take care of the church of God?" (TEV). Discuss this question with the children. What does it mean to them? Hang two pieces of posterboard on the wall. Label one "home" and the other "church." Have children cut out pictures and words from magazines and glue them onto the appropriate poster-board of how people can take care of home and how people can take care of church.

● **Find out who in your church is having radiation and chemotherapy treatments.** With the high incidences of cancer, large numbers of people require these treatments. Yet many are without the comforting support of family or friends. (If no one is currently having these treatments, find out who is recovering from surgery.) With the children, first make a "thinking of you" card for the person and then contact the person to arrange for the children to visit. Make a batch of cookies or brownies to take with you.

Helpful organizations

For the address, phone number, and web site of these organizations, see the Mission and Service Index starting on page 119.

● **Compassion International**—Sponsor a child in need through this organization. Often a classroom of children sponsors one child.

● **Kids Care Clubs**—Get ideas from all over the world of children who have formed Kids Care Clubs as a way to help others.

▪ Celebrate ▪

Too often we think of service and mission as hard work. And it can be hard work. Yet it's important hard work. An essential element of service and mission that tends to get overlooked is celebrating. Recognizing the achievements accomplished during projects and honoring them gives the participants a sense of completion and celebration.

After the Israelites crossed the Red Sea, they celebrated. Exodus 15:1-21 begins with a song from Moses, a song about how happy he is about getting through the Red Sea. Then Aaron's sister Miriam celebrates by singing her own song and playing her tambourine.

Celebrations inspire people—children and adults alike—to review what's been accomplished. Often celebrations give new energy to people and provide a sense of satisfaction for the work completed.

Ideas for 3- to 5-Year-olds

• **Exodus 23:14-19 highlights festivals and celebrations.** Read aloud verse 16: "Celebrate the Harvest Festival when you begin to harvest your crops. Celebrate the Festival of Shelters in the autumn, when you gather the fruit from your vineyards and orchards" (TEV). Give each child a two-foot piece of rolled crepe paper. (Ideally have four or more colors of rolled crepe paper and give each child a different color.) Talk about how children can celebrate all the hard work they've done so far. Put on music and have children dance, skip, and jump around the room as they wave their crepe paper.

• **When adults are doing a complex mission or service project (such as building a house for Habitat for Humanity), preschoolers can create celebration breaks by offering snacks on these workdays.** Set up free lemonade and cookie stands for children to man so they can give treats to the workers.

• **Young children can create a celebratory cheer to honor the accomplishments of those who do service and mission projects.** (This cheer can be done during a religious service or after the service project at the site.) Have children learn this cheer: Clap three times. Shout "Hooray." Clap three times. Shout "You made our day!" Clap three times. Shout "Good work done." Clap three times. Shout "Let's have some fun."

Ideas for 6- to 9-Year-olds

• **Read aloud the parable of the prodigal son in Luke 15:11-32.** Reread verses 23 and 24, which talk about having a celebration feast. Play hide-and-seek with only one child hiding while the rest of the children count to 20 before seeking out the child. Once the child is found, have the entire group give the child a celebratory group hug. Then play the game again with a different child hiding. Celebrate again when the child is found. Repeat the game until each child has had a chance to hide.

• **Throw a "welcome back" party to celebrate the arrival of people in your congregation returning from service or mission projects.** (Many churches have youth and/or adults who travel to mission sites for the weekend or a week.) Find out when the people will be returning and have a party waiting to celebrate the work they've done and their safe arrival home.

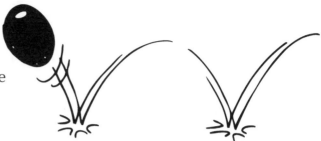

● **After children of this age finish a service or mission project, allow them to celebrate through play.** A game of kickball, kick-the-can, or tag often can be a great way for children to burn off excess energy and enjoy what they've accomplished. For children, playtime is always a way to celebrate.

Ideas for 10- to 12-Year-olds

● **Have children write haiku poetry to celebrate the service project they've completed.** A haiku is a Japanese poem that has three lines. The first line has five syllables, the second line has seven syllables. and the third line has five syllables. An example of a haiku poem celebrating a planting project:

We planted flowers.
Marigolds, Asters, Daisies
We celebrate now.

● **Discuss Nehemiah 8:1-12 where Ezra read the law of the people.** Have children study verses 10 and 12, where the people are encouraged to go home and celebrate in verse 10 and actually do so in verse 12. As a group, talk about what would be a meaningful celebration to mark the end of the year (or a major service or mission project) that's affordable and realistic. Then make plans to have this celebration at the appropriate time.

● **Learn a catchy celebratory hymn or song that your group can sing.** Some ideas: "Let All Things Now Living," "Come Ye Thankful People, Come," and "Now Thank We All Our God."

● **Create a congregation dessert cookbook.** Ask each member to donate a recipe card with her or his favorite dessert. Have children put together the recipes in a cookbook. Celebrate the project by giving each member a free cookbook at a congregation-wide dessert-fest.

Helpful organizations

For the address, phone number, and web site of these organizations, see the Mission and Service Index starting on page 119.

● **Kids Cheering Kids**—People from ages 5 to 23 work to create a better world for children who have less than they do. Children share their time, allowances, and optimism with others.

● **Special Olympics International**—This organization provides information about the special Olympic competitions for people with disabilities.

▪ Clean ▪

Cleaning is one way we take care of the things we have. We clean our homes. We clean our churches. We clean the out-of-doors. We clean all kinds of places. In John 13, Jesus washes the disciples' feet and makes a case for serving others. Cleaning serves others by removing clutter, brightening up a room, and giving something old the look of new life.

Ideas for 3- to 5-Year-olds

• **Teach preschoolers the first three words of Isaiah 1:16:** "Wash yourselves clean" (TEV). Talk about the importance of keeping ourselves and others clean. Talk about bathing, washing hair, and washing hands. After craft projects and snacks, have preschoolers team up and wash each other's hands in the sink while reciting the first three words of Isaiah 1:16.

• **Ask an adult volunteer to make magical mittens for preschoolers.** (Take two washcloths for each preschooler, pin them together, cut out an oversize mitten shape and sew together.) Give each preschooler a magical mitten to use to clean up tables after projects or to dust. Talk about the importance of helping out to keep things clean.

• **Volunteer to have preschoolers clean up the church sanctuary after a religious service, picking up bulletins and other papers left on the seats or pews.** Talk about the importance of keeping the sanctuary clean.

Ideas for 6- to 9-Year-olds

• **At the end of the Christian education year (or at the end of a Vacation Bible School or other special event) have children clean out the craft supplies.** Have them test markers and throw out those that no longer work. Have them separate the broken crayons from the unbroken crayons. Ask for volunteers to separate the construction paper into different sizes, the 8½-by-11-inch sheets into one pile, the 11-by-17-inch into another pile, and the scraps into another pile. Clean paint brushes. Refill glue bottles. Do whatever needs to be done to clean up the area for the next project.

• **Read aloud Job 37:21.** After a class project, have children act like the wind while they hurry and scurry to clean up the room. Explain that while the wind may be fast, it's not sloppy. It touches all areas and gets things clean.

• **On a warm day, clean the sports equipment for your church.** Often there are muddy or dirty balls, bats, plastic hockey sticks, and other items that are in need of cleaning. Take them all and clean them up with a hose. (Supervise children well so they clean appropriate items and don't get things too wet.) Have rags available to dry all the equipment afterward.

Ideas for 10- to 12-Year-olds

● **As a group, choose a playground to clean.** Pick up trash. Create a lost-and-found area for items that were left at the playground. Sweep all the sand or pea gravel off the slides and swings. Remove sticks, leaves, grass, and other debris from sandboxes.

● **Ask someone to read Matthew 23:25-28.** Discuss the point of the scripture, explaining how someone could look clean on the outside (such as having a clean face and clean clothes) but could be dirty on the inside because the person hits and yells at people. On the chalkboard or a flip chart make two lists: Outside and Inside. Have children brainstorm ideas of how they clean themselves in these two areas. Keeping things clean on the outside has to do with their outward appearances, such as washing their hair, cleaning under their fingernails, and wearing clean clothes. Inside cleaning tasks include developing

different Christian attributes, such as caring, forgiving, apologizing, and befriending. Afterward, have children choose an outside and an inside project they would like to focus on as a class. An idea for an outside project is for children to give a manicure to a person who is bedridden or to wash clothes for people at a homeless shelter. An idea for an inside project is each child apologizing to someone within the next week for something he or she hasn't apologized for yet.

● **Get involved in annual church cleanups.** (If your congregation doesn't have one of these days, have the children start one.) Children at this age can sweep floors, pick up trash, water plants, dust, and do other cleaning projects.

Helpful organizations

For the address, phone number, and web site of these organizations, see the Mission and Service Index starting on page 119.

● **Fresh Air Fund**—Advocate for clean air through this organization.

● **Giraffe Project**—This organization encourages children and adults to "stick their necks out" to make the world a better place by working on projects such as pollution, hunger, and violence.

▪ Collect ▪

First Corinthians 16:1-2 calls us to collect things to give away. "Now about the collection for God's people: Do what I told the Galatian churches to do. On the first day of every week, each one of you should set aside a sum of money in keeping with his income" (NIV). While monetary gifts are important to collect, so are the things that money buys: things like sweaters, nonperishable food, blankets, and so on. Almost anything can be collected for any group of people, although some items are easier for certain age groups of children to collect than others.

Ideas for All Children

● **Ask children to bring in gently used toys and books to give away.** Any age child can do this, and it's often a good challenge for children to come up with a number of items from their rooms to give away. With preschoolers, ask them to bring in one or two things. With older children, challenge them to bring in four or five. After children bring in these items, ask them how hard this was for them to do and why they think it's important to give away some of the things they own.

● **During special churchwide collection drives, create a list with four or five items that would be of interest to children.** Distribute these lists to Christian education classes and encourage children to shop for one item (of their choice) with their parents. This activity empowers children by giving them choices so they can contribute in ways that fit their interests.

● **Have a baby-food drive where you collect boxes and jars of baby food to give to low-income families and community agencies that provide services for low-income families.**

Ideas for 3- to 5-Year-olds

● **When your church is collecting items for kits where each bag has exactly the same items, such as first-aid kits, back-to-school supplies, or baby kits, give preschoolers the task of dropping the items into the bags.** Supervise preschoolers as they do this since they can become distracted and drop two of the same item into one bag or skip a bag. Most of the time, preschoolers will find this task exciting, challenging, and meaningful.

● **Talk about how the Bible says it's good to collect things to help others (Genesis 41:35-36).** Contact a local agency or community volunteer organization that serves preschoolers. Find out which items your preschoolers could collect, such as toys that preschoolers like, clothing, and everyday essentials (for example, toothbrushes and toothpaste). Be creative with your service-project collection.

For example, if you're collecting clothing, collect one type of clothing, such as shoes, hats, or underwear. (Children often get a big kick out of collecting preschool underwear, and many will encourage their parents to bring ones with colorful designs or popular figures on them.)

● **Encourage preschoolers to give by collecting an offering each week.** Make it a penny offering or a nickel and penny offering. Educate parents on the importance of starting children early on the road to giving. After you collect the offering each week, count the money with the preschoolers so they can see how pennies can add up—even if each child only brings one or two. Consider giving the pennies to Common Cents New York, an organization that accepts penny donations for the homeless.

Ideas for 6- to 9-Year-olds

● **Hang a clothesline.** Have children create a pair of paper mittens by tracing their hands on construction paper. Ask children to cut out the mittens. Hang the paper mittens from the clothesline. Challenge the children (and the adults of your congregation) to replace the paper mittens with real mittens to give to children who may not have them. The clothesline can be hung in a classroom, a narthex, or even a sanctuary.

● **Talk about how collecting can take a long time and that the people of Judea once spent three whole days collecting clothes, supplies, and other valuables.** Discuss with the children that even after three days, there was a lot more that they could still collect (2 Chronicles 20:25-26). Partner with an elementary school and find out which teachers collect used items, such as empty egg cartons, old magazines, empty paper towel rolls, etc., for classroom use. Have children collect these items. As a group, take these items to the school and meet the teacher. Ask the teacher (arrange this beforehand) to show the children how these items will be used.

● **Work with a local agency or community volunteer office to create "giving trees" at Christmastime.** Cut a large Christmas tree out of green construction paper. Cut out and hang construction paper ball ornaments on the tree. Ask the agency to identify ten children who otherwise wouldn't get anything—or much—for Christmas. Have the agency write the first name of each child and one to two gift ideas on each ornament. Tape the ornaments to the tree. Have children and parents take an ornament if they wish and buy a Christmas present for that child to bring to the church and place under the tree. Arrange with the agency a deadline for delivering all of the items.

Ideas for 10- to 12-Year-olds

- **Children of this age enjoy creating collection kits that are more complex, such as back-to-school supply kits for children who otherwise couldn't afford school supplies, emergency kits (with flashlights, batteries, matches, and a candle), or bill-paying kits (with stamps, envelopes, pens, and stationery).** Children enjoy creating the list for the kits, collecting the items, assembling the items, and even decorating the containers to place the items in.

- **Give children UNICEF collection boxes before Halloween to collect coins from people in addition to treats.** This encourages children to think of others—in addition to themselves—on Halloween. Prior to Halloween, have children read Romans 12:8: "Whoever shares with others should do it generously" (TEV). Discuss the importance of being generous when collecting things.

- **Have children collect soda cans, soup labels, cereal box tops, or other items that earn money.** Cereal manufacturers, soup manufacturers, and others often offer these programs. Contact the public relations office of the manufacturer for details. Challenge children to collect a certain number of these items before turning them in. Creatively display what children bring in so children can see their progress. For example, create a wall chart that shows the collections to date compared to the end goal. When the end goal is reached, have the group brainstorm and choose a worthwhile charity to give the money to.

Helpful organizations

For the address, phone number, and web site of these organizations, see the Mission and Service Index starting on page 119.

- **Common Cents New York Inc.**—This organization accepts collections of pennies that are then given to the homeless. The organization collected $103,268.68 for the homeless in the first year it was founded.

- **UNICEF**—This organization has collection boxes for Halloween and also other ways for children to do collections that make a difference for children in need.

▪ Cook ▪

Cooking and eating may seem like ordinary events, but they are often at the center of radical situations in scripture. Throughout Jesus' life, Christ was criticized for whom he ate with. In Mark 2:13-17, the Pharisees weren't happy about Jesus eating with the outcasts and tax collectors. Even when Jesus asked Zacchaeus to come down from the tree in Luke 19, he told Zacchaeus to hurry home because Jesus was coming to stay—which meant he was coming to eat.

The Lord's Supper is a table that's inviting, just like the tables we have in our homes. We invite family members to come together and eat. But not only are eating times sacred, so are cooking times, like the ones mentioned in Zechariah 14:20-21. Cooking and providing food for others is a way to meet their everyday needs of nourishment and fellowship.

Ideas for 3- to 5-Year-olds

• **Make sugar cookies for preschoolers to decorate with sprinkles, candy, and other toppings.** Often you can find a premade sugar cookie in the refrigerated section of your grocery store and cut the premade batter into portions so that most of the time is spent with children decorating the cookies instead of mixing the ingredients. Afterward, give the cookies to people you deem would benefit most. Maybe it's families with newborns, shut-ins, or a church committee that has been working long hours lately.

• **Simplify the story of Exodus 2:16-22 of Moses hiding and having people seek him out to invite him to eat.** Children at this age often can relate to this story since some hide at meal times. Talk about the importance of eating together, even when people aren't hungry. What we want are times to gather to talk together. Emphasize this point every time you have a snack. Even if children aren't hungry, encourage them to come to the table just to talk.

• **As a group make simple drinks, such as lemonade, limeade, Kool-Aid, or juice.** Team up with older children who can pour the drinks into cups to serve at a church function, such as an annual church picnic, or at a service project.

Ideas for 6- to 9-Year-olds

• **Read aloud Mark 6:30-44 about Jesus feeding the five thousand.** Ask children how they think five loaves and two fish were able to feed all those people.

Have an unfrosted cake donut, bagel, or bread roll for children to pass around. Encourage children to take a little bit to eat and share so that everyone has something to eat. Before you actually do this, have children guess whether they think everyone can have a little bit to eat. Ask how many times it will take before it's completely gone. See how close children's guesses are to reality.

• **Make sandwiches to take to a homeless shelter or soup kitchen.** (Check with the organization first to make sure sandwiches are something they can use.) Children can make a variety of sandwiches: peanut butter and jelly, bologna, cheese, turkey, and so on. Make sandwiches that won't spoil easily. Adding lettuce and tomato often leads to quick spoilage, so talk about how difficult it is to make nutritious meals when you have to be concerned about spoilage. Have children deliver the sandwiches and, if possible, serve them.

• **Have children make salads for a church dinner.** While children will need adult help with cutting vegetables, they can tear lettuce and assemble ingredients into salad bowls.

Ideas for 10- to 12-Year-olds

• **Borrow a bread maker and make loaves of bread with children.** Eat the first loaf and bake bread to give to other people. Some churches give a loaf of bread to people who visit the church, saying they want to break bread together again with them in the future.

• **Study Genesis 27:1-10, focusing on the significance of cooking and food in the story.** As a group, make a pizza together, getting a premade pizza crust and adding the toppings. Bake and then eat. Talk about how cooking together and eating together is an act of service to one another.

• **Together make cookies, bars, brownies, and other easy desserts to celebrate young people's confirmation or graduation.** These churchwide celebrations often need items made, and children at this age can work together to bake them.

Helpful organizations

For the address, phone number, and web site of these organizations, see the Mission and Service Index starting on page 119.

• **Food Works**—School and community gardens provide food for the hungry through this organization.

• **U.S. National Committee for the World Food Day**—This organization has projects that children can be involved in for World Food Day.

• Create •

The Bible begins with the intricate Creation story in Genesis 1—a story about creating something out of nothing, creating something that's useful and meaningful.

It's important to use creativity in service and mission projects. Too often, it's easy to approach these types of projects with the intent of simply repeating what was done before or what worked before. Yet, in reality, the most powerful projects are ones that are unique, personal, and creative.

Ideas for 3- to 5-Year-olds

- **Talk about how God created everything, using the passage from Colossians 1:16.** Whenever you make crafts and projects together, before getting started encourage the children to think of someone to give the project to as a gift. Often this adds new enthusiasm to doing crafts—or even to drawing a picture. Or consider having the children make something for each other. For example, each child could make a picture for the person on her or his right.
- **Preschoolers often have great ideas for ways to adapt a favorite game.** Try their ideas and keep adjusting until the new adaptation works well. Then have preschoolers teach the game to another class in your church. Or have preschoolers teach the game to children in another class or children who attend a child-care center or program.
- **Make placemats out of 11-by-17-inch construction paper and have them laminated after preschoolers decorate them with crayons, markers, paints, and/or stickers.** Give these creations to senior citizen centers and nursing homes or use them for your church dinners.

Ideas for 6- to 9-Year-olds

- **Have children learn Psalm 139:13:** "You created every part of me; you put me together in my mother's womb" (TEV). Examine how creative God is by learning about all the different people God has made. Arrange for your group to do a project with a group of children who are different from them: a group of either a different race, socioeconomic group, religion, or culture. Together make a poster of an ideal world for children, creating their vision on posterboard or some other type of medium.
- **Ask children to draw pictures of happy families.** Frame them or give them construction-paper backing (so that it looks like a frame). Donate these pictures to a Ronald McDonald House, hospital, or other place where children often feel separated from their families for a while.

• **Have children think of themselves as angels and brainstorm angel-like activities they could do when you visit someone who is housebound or bedridden.** (Ideas could include bringing flowers or cookies, playing a game with the person, sending a card to the person afterward, asking the person questions about her or his life, and so on.) Afterward, give children angel wings, angel halos, or angel stickers to thank them for their thoughtfulness.

Ideas for 10- to 12-Year-olds

• **As a group, study Ephesians 4:17-24.** Encourage children to memorize Ephesians 4:24, "Put on the new self, which is created in God's likeness and reveals itself in the true life that is upright and holy" (TEV). Have children take a new creation quiz and rank their strongest qualities in order. (Have them rank qualities such as caring, giving, helping, creating, planning, organizing, learning, playing, visiting, and welcoming.) Then have them star the one quality they would like to develop more in themselves. Discuss how doing service and mission projects gives young people the opportunity not only to serve but also to develop into the people they want to become.

• **Encourage children to create service projects based on the type of food that is in season.** In winter, you can make orange juice and orange shakes. In fall, apple pie, apple crisp, apple juice, and apple strudel would be appropriate. In summer, create a berry festival and deliver pints of blueberries, raspberries, blackberries, or strawberries to people who otherwise might not get them. In spring, collect and donate jars of honey and give a jar with a single carnation flower as symbols of hope, new life, and sweetness.

• **Create a mission tree to display in the main foyer of your church.** (Ask for permission first.) Make a tree trunk out of large brown paper, about three or four feet high. Cut green, yellow, orange, and red leaves out of construction paper. Have children write one idea of how to be service-minded on each leaf. Ideas could include talking to people, sending a card to someone, calling someone on the phone, running an errand for someone, inviting someone to dinner, visiting someone, taking flowers to someone, and so on. Encourage children to fill the tree full of leaves. Consider calling this the giving tree, and read Shel Silverstein's book *The Giving Tree*.[1]

Helpful organizations

For the address, phone number, and web site of these organizations, see the Mission and Service Index starting on page 119.

• **Kids for Saving Earth (KSE)**—A kids' environmental action club, this organization publishes a newsletter on how kids can save the earth.

• **Oxfam America**—Create a better world where poverty no longer has the impact that it currently does.

• Deliver •

An essential component of service and mission projects is the act of delivering items to service project sites or to people who need certain items. This is often an overlooked, nonglamorous task, yet it is an essential one.

Nehemiah 3:17-32 highlights the essential role every person had in rebuilding the wall of Jerusalem. This scripture passage lists every person and what that person did. All roles are vital in service and mission projects. The one who delivers the meal to someone who is homebound or bedridden is just as important as the cook.

Ideas for 3- to 5-Year-olds

• **Role-play the story in Mark 2:1-12.** Tie yarn, string, or rope to the four ends of a bath towel, making sure that the four pieces of yarn are all the same length. Place a stuffed animal onto the towel. Ask for four volunteers. Have the other children sit in a circle. Have the four volunteers stand outside the circle and gently lower the stuffed animal in the towel into the middle of the circle. Talk about the story and the important part the four people had in delivering the man to Jesus to be healed. Point out how we help sick people today by taking them to the doctor or the hospital, by going to the pharmacy to pick up medicine, and by visiting them when they're sick. These are all important things to do.

• **On the last Sunday before the end of the school year, have preschoolers deliver a flower, thank-you note, or some other small token to give to each teacher during the education hour.**

• **At a church banquet, dinner, or other sit-down meal, have preschoolers offer wrapped mints or chocolates to those sitting at each table.** (Having wrapped candy is ideal in case children drop them since they're protected; using small plastic bowls that are easier for children to handle also helps them succeed in this task.)

Ideas for 6- to 9-Year-olds

• **Discuss Numbers 1:47-54, which talks about how the people called the Levites had the important role of bringing the tabernacle to a new place.** Since there weren't cars or trucks back then, the only way they had to deliver the tabernacle was to carry it. After you discuss the scripture, find a small meaningful, moving project within your church or classroom to show children why moving items from one place to another is an important task. For example, maybe you want to make your room more accessible for children by rearranging it. Maybe your church wants to combine the small libraries that each classroom has into an all-church library in a certain room. Children can carry items from one place to another.

- **During teacher training or a teacher workshop, have children round up the supplies that each teacher will need for the coming months or school year.** Have children load the supplies into wagons and deliver them to each classroom.

- **When you do canned food or toy collection drives, arrange for transportation so that children can actually deliver these items.** Too often, children only collect items and never get to see where these items are taken. After a delivery is made, visit with the person in order to give children more of the experience of interacting with the people they serve.

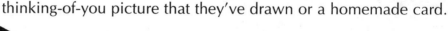

Ideas for 10- to 12-Year-olds

- **Take children grocery shopping to buy items for a church member who may be homebound or bedridden.** After making your purchase, with the children deliver the items to the person and spend a little time visiting the person.

- **As a group, study Luke 11:46-51.** Discuss why Jesus is so angry. Talk about what we can learn from this passage. Together research who are the drivers and errand runners of your church and create a thank-you note or some type of recognition to present to these individuals during worship. (Children also can write short paragraphs about what each individual does for your church bulletin or church newsletter.)

- **Have children accompany adult and teenage drivers (after you have permission from their parents) when delivering meals to people who are homebound or bedridden.** Children can also take a thinking-of-you picture that they've drawn or a homemade card.

Helpful organizations

For the address, phone number, and web site of these organizations, see the Mission and Service Index starting on page 119.

- **Food for the Hungry**—Help the hungry become self-supporting through the work of this organization, which also provides disaster relief.

- **Meals on Wheels**—This organization arranges for meals to be delivered to the homes of people who are no longer able to cook for themselves.

▪ Educate ▪

Often service grows out of new information and knowledge. We hear about the atrocities that occur during a war and suddenly we can create a wide variety of ways to serve people in a part of the world that most of us hadn't heard about until the war broke out. The same is true about various diseases, injustices, and other inhumane treatment that people and animals endure.

Romans 12:1-8 encourages us to use our gifts and to use them to the fullest. Verse 7 says, "If it is to serve, we should serve; if it is to teach, we should teach" (TEV). Educate children about various issues to help them know about the needs of our world.

Ideas for 3- to 5-Year-olds

● **Talk about Psalm 25:4-5 and how we need others to teach us to know what's right and how to live as Christians.** Sit in a circle and go around and have children tell about the most important thing their moms taught them. Be sensitive to the family situations of the children. For example, if you have several children who live in one-parent families or alternate family situations, it may be wise to substitute "parent" or "guardian" for "mom." Then go around the circle again and ask about someone else (such as a dad, grandma, grandpa, aunt, uncle, family friend, etc.). Next, ask each child what he or she has been taught about helping.

● **Teach preschoolers about one or two of the different programs that your church has that would be interesting to this age group.** Usually a group that does something besides talk would be of interest to preschoolers. For example, do you have a sewing circle, a choir, or a softball team? Have children visit that group to learn a little more about it. When you return, identify one way you can support and serve the group. Then do it.

● **As a group, learn about one of the mission or service projects or community outreach emphases that your congregation currently has.** (If your church doesn't have one, find out about one in your community through United Way or another volunteer group.) Find a way to involve preschoolers in meaningful service for that project so that they feel included and also feel like they're contributing. For example, if your church is sending a group of teenagers to a work camp or mission trip, preschoolers can make a "Have a Great Trip" sign to send them off. Banners can be made from paper, fabric, or cardboard.

Ideas for 6- to 9-Year-olds

● **Help children learn about the mission field or missionary that your church supports.** Give them experiential activities, such as sampling food from that country, learning a song or game from that country, and locating the country on a map. If the missionary should visit your church, arrange for that person to visit with the children to help make this work more concrete and personal to them.

• **Teach children Psalm 27:11:** "Teach me, LORD, what you want me to do, and lead me along a safe path" (TEV). As a group, have children take turns naming their favorite Bible story and what that story has taught them. Ask each child to draw a picture of their favorite Bible story and then make a display, labeled as "Best Bible Teaching." Write about this display in your church newsletter or bulletin, encouraging others to visit the display and think about the Bible story that has had the most profound influence on their faith.

• **Learn about the needs of your communities around the holidays.** For example, some communities offer a Thanksgiving dinner to those who can't afford one. Other communities make Easter baskets for homeless children. Contact the organizers of one of these projects to find out how your children can participate.

Ideas for 10- to 12-Year-olds

• **Teach children your church's mission statement or the creed.** Based on the statement or creed, have the group identify service projects that would allow that statement to be one of action.

• **Discuss Proverbs 6:20-23.** Emphasize verse 22: "Their teaching will lead you when you travel, protect you at night, and advise you during the day" (TEV). Ask each child to identify the teacher (a school teacher or church teacher) who has made the most impact on them. Have each child write a thank-you letter to that teacher that tells how much that person means to them. Work with children to identify how to locate these people so you can mail the letters.

• **Have children look at the list of organizations listed in the Mission and Service Index on pages 119-24.** As a group, identify two or three that the group would like to learn more about. Write to these groups, requesting information about their organizations. After the materials arrive, study them as a group and decide which ones lend themselves to service projects that they can do.

• **Create a hunger calendar using a blank calendar page.** Write a specific action that children are to do daily as a way to raise money for a hunger organization or food bank. Include actions such as: Give 5¢ for every bed you have in your house. Give 1¢ for every shoe in your house. Give 2¢ for each can of food in your cupboard. Use this activity not only to encourage children to give money but also to educate them about hunger issues.

Helpful organizations

For the address, phone number, and web site of these organizations, see the Mission and Service Index starting on page 119.

• **Children's Rainforest**—Donate to help save Costa Rica's rain forest through the Children's Project of this organization.

• **Prevent Child Abuse America**—An educational clearinghouse, this organization offers information about all the various forms of child abuse.

▪ Entertain ▪

Part of hospitality and service involves entertaining people. We can entertain others through music, plays, puppets, dance, reading, clowning, telling funny and appropriate jokes, talking with them, or giving a speech at a banquet. Entertaining is a way of lifting people's spirits, which is another way to serve others.

Psalms 148–150 tell of the many ways to make an impact, from trumpets to dancing to loud cymbals. While this scripture emphasizes the enthusiasm and loudness of doing this, entertaining others through the spirit of service can be quiet or loud. What's essential is to identify ways to raise people's spirits and hopes.

Ideas for 3- to 5-Year-olds

• **Have preschoolers put on a program for parents (or some other group of people in your congregation or community).** Include different ways for them to entertain others, such as: speaking (for example, children standing in a row and saying their names and what they like best about church), performing a simple dance, and so on. Make the program short and varied, with roles that preschoolers can master.

• **Discuss Isaiah 12:4-6 with preschoolers, talking about how singing is a good way to serve people.** As a group, learn a song that the children enjoy. (Usually a song that involves easy instruments like sticks and drums or one that gets children moving is one this age group will like.) Then perform the song during a religious service, a mother-daughter banquet, or an all-church dinner.

• **During worship, have preschoolers do a short speaking part and/or clapping part.** For example, you can create a litany where preschoolers say "Praise the Lord" whenever you pause. (Have an adult stand in front of the children to help signal when children are supposed to say their part in the reading.) Giving preschoolers opportunities to do simple things as a group in front of people will help give them confidence so that they are not shy about doing things in front of groups or meeting new people on service projects.

Ideas for 6- to 9-Year-olds

• **If your youth group or an adult group does a play each year (for instance, a congregation may reenact the Christmas story each December), find a role for children.** For example, children can create an angel choir for the Christmas story and sing "Away in a Manger" for the performance.

• **Point out how 2 Samuel 6:12-15 is about eating, dancing, and making music as part of bringing the Covenant Box to Jerusalem.** Invite someone from your congregation or your community to teach children simple magic tricks that they can perform for their families and friends. As children become more adept at these tricks, have them perform these tricks when you are doing service projects.

• Have children create a simple puppet show that they can present to the preschool children in your church. Help them choose or write a script. Find puppets for them to use. Some children may get so interested that they'll want to make the background scenery or create programs and tickets.

Ideas for 10- to 12-Year-olds

• Study Hebrews 13:1-2: "Keep on loving one another as Christians. Remember to welcome strangers in your homes. There were some who did that and welcomed angels without knowing it" (TEV). Talk about how welcoming people includes making them feel comfortable. Often times when people welcome visitors, they do something that entertains the guest. For example, someone may play music, while others may share some poetry or a book they've read. Together identify how your group can entertain guests and newcomers to your class. For example, maybe you'll have a welcome song or a favorite class game to teach the person. Make this a tradition that you use only when you have visitors and first-time newcomers.

• Have children create a congregational joke book with favorite jokes from children and adults in the congregation. (Be clear about what's appropriate for inclusion in this book.) Then make copies for people to have or sell copies to raise money for a charitable cause. Children can unveil the new book at a church function.

• Invite someone from your congregation or community who can teach children simple juggling. As children practice their skill, find outlets for them to share these skills, such as at a church picnic, by visiting a nursing home, or as part of a worship service.

Helpful organizations

For the address, phone number, and web site of these organizations, see the Mission and Service Index starting on page 119.

• **Puppeteers of America**—Amateur and professional puppeteers (along with those who are just interested in puppeteering) can learn helpful information through this organization.

• **YMCA of the USA**—In addition to providing entertaining programs for children, youth, and adults, this organization also has recreational, educational, and social programs.

• Fight Crime •

Keeping people safe is something we all value and is a topic that's addressed in scripture. In Hosea 2:14-23, God speaks of loving people by providing safety. "At that time I will make a covenant with all the wild animals and birds, so that they will not harm my people. I will also remove all weapons of wars from the land, all swords and bows, and will let my people live in peace and safety" (Hosea 2:18 TEV).

An important aspect of service is creating safe homes and neighborhoods, places of refuge for people to live and thrive. Although we have law enforcement to fight crime, the communities that are most safe are ones where each person does her or his part in making a safe community. Safety is an important value. It's another way that children can serve.

Ideas for 3- to 5-Year-olds

● **Teach children their last name in addition to their first name, their address, and their phone number.** Since numbers are difficult for preschoolers to remember, set them to music that has seven beats, such as "Twinkle, Twinkle Little Star" and "The Itsy-Bitsy Spider." Talk about how preschoolers can fight crime by keeping themselves safe and knowing this information.

● **Talk about how Jesus protects us and keeps us safe, which is the central message of John 17:12.** Tell children the story of the lost sheep in Luke 15:1-7. After you read the story, act out the story, having one child play Jesus, another the lost sheep, and all the other children the sheep. Have the lost sheep hide away from the group. Then have everyone come in. Have all the other sheep pretend to eat and have Jesus go looking for the lost sheep to bring it back to the group.

● **Ask preschoolers to draw a picture of what scares them the most.** (Often preschoolers are afraid of monsters and animals.) Instill in them a sense of personal safety and power by having them say "You don't scare me" and ripping up the picture and throwing it away. As a group, read the book *Go Away, Big Green Monster!* by Ed Emberley.[2] Then create safe pairs where each child has a partner in class. Each partner is to be a safety guide for the other, alerting a grownup right away if the other child gets hurt or feels scared or sad.

Ideas for 6- to 9-Year-olds

● **Celebrate Baby Safety Month in September[3] by having your group play with infants in the nursery one time during the month, and distribute infant safety information to parents as the parents pick up their children.** (You can often get free infant safety information from your local police station or safety council.)

- **Ask someone to read aloud Proverbs 28:26:** "It is foolish to follow your own opinions. Be safe, and follow the teachings of wiser people" (TEV). As a group, discuss the ways in which safety and learning are connected. Invite a police officer or some other safety expert from your community to speak to the group about ways they can keep themselves and other people in the community safe. As a group, choose one action to do that will make your community a safer place.
- **Get rid of graffiti by organizing a painting day.** Some congregations have created groups of children that immediately paint over graffiti as soon as it appears.

Ideas for 10- to 12-Year-olds

- **Study Psalm 12:6-8.** Ask children to memorize Psalm 12:8: "Keep us always safe, O LORD, and preserve us from such people" (TEV). Have children create a safety survey to give to people in your congregation or people in your neighborhood to find out their safety concerns and which crimes they're most afraid of. Publish the results of the survey and then work to create a safe community by helping people get to know each other. Law enforcement officials often cite strong community and strong relationships as a key to crime prevention.
- **Create a donation drive of safety items for families who cannot afford them.** Have a collection for car seats, bike helmets, smoke detectors, or carbon monoxide detectors.
- **As a group, stay aware of crime in your church or your neighborhood.** As a service project, alert others as soon as a crime has been committed. For example, if a purse has been stolen in your church, either make an announcement to the congregation alerting them to the situation or create some written flyer to distribute. Telling others about a crime makes others aware of the need to be more careful. It also shows criminals that you have zero tolerance for crime in your church or neighborhood. Whenever children alert others about a crime, make sure they do so within the context that this is one crime and that the purpose of telling others is to make everyone safe, not to scare people. Encourage children to help others to empower themselves against future crime.

Helpful organizations

For the address, phone number, and web site of these organizations, see the Mission and Service Index starting on page 119.
- **National Crime Prevention Council**—Build safer, more caring communities by finding out how to prevent crime through this organization.
- **National Safe Kids Campaign**—This national campaign advocates that all children be safe from crime and abuse.

· Give ·

Giving through service is a broad category. There are four major styles of giving. We can give of our *money*. We can give of our *time*. We can give of our *talents and gifts*. We can give of *what we already own*. Often it's helpful to learn about all these different styles of giving and to challenge children to give in these different ways.

Giving is a central message of scripture. "Then the King will say to the people on his right, 'Come, you that are blessed by my Father! Come and possess the kingdom which has been prepared for you ever since the creation of the world. I was hungry and you fed me, thirsty and you gave me a drink; I was a stranger and you received me in your homes, naked and you clothed me; I was sick and you took care of me, in prison and you visited me.'... The King will reply, 'I tell you whenever you did this for one of the least important of these followers of mine, you did it for me!' " (Matthew 25:34-36, 40 TEV).

Ideas for 3- to 5-Year-olds

● **Make a giving coupon or certificate on which children can write their names (or have you help them write their names) to give to their parents.** The coupon or certificate is good for one act of giving by the child, such as picking up toys, putting napkins on the table at mealtime, or giving a sibling an extra hug. At your group's next meeting, ask about how these experiences went by holding up the coupon or certificate as a visual reminder.

● **Discuss how the Bible is filled with stories about people and their giving.** For example, Ezra 8:24-30 lists what people gave, and all these were good gifts. Ask children to talk about the gifts they've given, such as gifts for a birthday party, for Mother's or Father's Day, for Christmas, or for some other event. Although most children at this age are more interested in receiving than in giving gifts, begin to emphasize the point of giving. Talking about the gifts they gave helps preschoolers practice thinking about others.

● **Get a small, clear glass jar with a lid and call it the giving jar.** Each week, encourage preschoolers to bring coins for the giving jar. (Send home a note to parents about this giving jar.) Bring the jar out each week and let children add their money to the giving jar. (The clear glass will help children see how the money grows each week.) When the jar is full, ask children for ideas on who should receive the money. As a group, present the jar to the organization or committee.

Ideas for 6- to 9-Year-olds

● **Create a giving chain by cutting construction-paper strips and using markers and a stapler to create the chain.** Each week, give each child a construction-paper slip and a marker. Have them write their name on the slip and tell the group one act of giving they did in the past week while they attach their slip to the chain. After a month (or a year, if you want to keep it going that long), you'll have a visual reminder of how small acts of giving can add up when linked with others.

- **Read aloud the story of Luke 21:1-4 about the generous widow's offering.** During your time together, institute an offering each time to encourage children to bring money and give. Talk about how even giving one coin is a good start and that it often takes a number of times to get into the habit of giving money on a regular basis since it's easy to be forgetful at first. Send home reminders to parents and stick with the offering, even if few children participate. What's important is to encourage the habit and to keep promoting it.

- **Show the power of pennies by encouraging children to set up a congregation-wide penny fund-raiser for a cause they have chosen.** For example, Central United Methodist Church in North Carolina had a "Mile of Pennies" challenge during a vacation church school. With the help of church members, it took children seven months to raise 84,480 pennies ($844.80) to reach the one-mile mark.[4]

Ideas for 10- to 12-Year-olds

- **Have children research and create a list of all the major programs and activities of your congregation.** Identify the commitment required in terms of time, talent, and money. Expand opportunities for children, if need be. Distribute this list or booklet for everyone in the congregation. Have children encourage people to give of their time and talents.

- **Talk about Ezekiel 18:1-9, emphasizing verse 7.** This passage is about taking individual responsibility, which includes giving. Encourage children to make pledges during your church's annual stewardship drives and to give to special offerings throughout the year, even if they're giving only loose change. (Then advocate for the stewardship committee to be more inclusive so that people of all ages—even young children—are encouraged and challenged to give during stewardship drives and special offerings.)

- **Have children write an article for your church's newsletter or bulletin on how your congregation is living out its commitment of giving.** Go with children to interview people on the finance, stewardship, and mission committees. Work with them to refine the article for publication. Also consider submitting a similar article for publication in your community newspaper, too.

Helpful organizations

For the address, phone number, and web site of these organizations, see the Mission and Service Index starting on page 119.

- **Goodwill Industries of America Inc.**—Giving monetary and noncash donations to this organization allows it to provide leadership and education for people with disabilities and other barriers to employment.

- **The Hole in the Wall Gang Fund**—This camp caters to children with serious health problems.

▪ Grant Wishes ▪

First Timothy 6:18 encourages us to "do good, to be rich in good works, to be generous and ready to share with others" (TEV). A key way to provide service for others is to meet their needs. Yet, it's often tempting to make assumptions and to serve others in the way we think would be best.

Organizations such as the Make-a-Wish Foundation and the Starlight Children's Foundation are known for granting the wishes of children who are terminally or chronically ill. Couldn't more people benefit from doing service in this way? What are the wishes of the elderly? People with disabilities? People living on low incomes? What could children do to make these wishes come true?

Ideas for 3- to 5-Year-olds

• **Talk with people who receive monthly income assistance or have low incomes (or with coordinators who work in programs that serve them) to find out which shopping items are on their wish list.** (Food stamps are usually restrictive in terms of what people are allowed to buy.) Preschoolers can go shopping and deliver these items.

• **Teach children about Matthew 5:14-16 so that they know that they are the light of the world.** Make your classroom dark and have the children be very quiet. Then turn on a flashlight or light one candle. Talk about how one small light makes a big difference in the darkness. Explain that you're all going to be a light to your church's Christian education coordinator. Make a group card with a candle on it, writing the words "You are the light of our education program" and place it in the coordinator's office (or mail box) with a dozen cookies.

• **Be in charge of filling up bird feeders and bird baths for your church.** If your church doesn't have any bird feeders, see if you can work with some older children, teenagers, or adults who would be interested in putting some up. Then have your preschoolers keep the feeders filled throughout the year.

Ideas for 6- to 9-Year-olds

• **Read aloud Proverbs 18:16:** "Do you want to meet an important person? Take a gift and it will be easy" (TEV). Talk about why this is true. Ask: Does this mean all people are important? Why or why not? Why does a gift make it easy? Many people who work in custodial services rarely receive feedback from people, and they often work at times when people aren't around. Make thank-you baskets for the people who perform janitorial services for your congregation. Include candy, fruit, and a thank-you note that says why children appreciate the good work they do.

● **Request a list of needed items from a local service agency (such as a homeless shelter or food bank) and start a service project to educate the congregation about these needs.** Then create a plan to fulfill those needs through cash donations and the collection of these items.

● **Talk with expectant parents (particularly during the third trimester) and parents of newborns to see what wishes they have.** Sometimes an expectant mother has to have bed rest or a parent of a newborn needs extra support because of a husband who travels. Be creative in meeting these needs.

Ideas for 10- to 12-Year-olds

● **Ask your church paid staff what wishes they have that would make either their work or their personal lives a little bit easier.** (Children can interview staff—or you can have an adult ask staff.) Then create a service project to make those wishes come true, even if you can only do something small, such as washing the cars of all the paid staff when they're working and surprising them.

● **By talking with children and adults with permanent hair loss (either through injury, burns, or a medical condition known as alopecia), a child named Peggy Knight learned that many families can't afford natural wigs.** So she started "Locks of Love," a program where people donated a minimum of ten inches of their own hair to be made into natural wigs.[5]

● **Study 2 Corinthians 8:7:** "You are so rich in all you have: in faith, speech, and knowledge, in your eagerness to help and in your love for us. And so we want you to be generous also in this service of love" (TEV). Do your children feel rich in all they have? Why or why not? Have them read 2 Corinthians 8:1-7 to put this scripture passage into context. Now what do they think of this message? How does this fit with their lives today? Talk to the family of someone who is chronically or terminally ill in your church or community. What one wish does the family have—a wish that seems like an impossibility? (For example, buying a wheelchair often seems like an unreachable dream for some families.) As a group, figure out a way to meet that need.

Helpful organizations

For the address, phone number, and web site of these organizations, see the Mission and Service Index starting on page 119.

● **Make-a-Wish Foundation**—This organization grants the wishes of children who are terminally ill.

● **Starlight Children's Foundation**—Children who are seriously ill can have their wishes fulfilled through this organization.

· Heal ·

Throughout scripture, many passages emphasize the value of healing others (1 Corinthians 12:27-31). In fact, a lot of Jesus' ministry centered around healing. Mark 1:29-34 gives the overview of how Jesus healed many people, people who had a wide variety of diseases.

People who are sick often talk about the healing nature of children, how their presence often soothes their souls and bandages their broken hearts. Children have a spontaneous enthusiasm about them that reminds people about the goodness of life. It's of great service for children to be involved in the act of healing.

Ideas for All children

• **Have children collect donations of tissue boxes and put them in each room of your church.** Some churches even encourage children to each bring one box of tissues at the beginning of the Christian education year for this purpose.

• **Raise funds to arrange for free immunizations one day at your church or community center for families who may not be able to afford these important shots.** Children can help promote the service by giving flyers to individuals in the congregation and by going with adults to drop off a stack of flyers at social-service agencies.

• **Request information from UNICEF about how a little money can make a big difference in the health of a person in a developing country.** For example, UNICEF lists how different amounts of coins (usually less than a dollar) will pay for essential medical services, such as oral rehydration therapy where sterilized water and sugar are given to malnourished children to rehydrate them. Have children bring in coins to raise money for specific health needs.

Ideas for 3- to 5-year-olds

• **Create a bandage kit for your class filled with a variety of bandages (not only of different sizes but also of different characters and designs).** Preschoolers love bandages, and can help each other put on bandages when cuts and scrapes occur.

• **Talk about how Jesus spent a lot of time healing people and how the Bible is filled with stories about healing, such as in Matthew 8:1-13.** Create a cough-drop container for the narthex of your church, encouraging people who attend worship services to help themselves if they have a cough. (Your pastor may think this is a great service!) Preschoolers can then keep tabs on the container and keep it filled.

• **Have preschoolers role-play doctor.** Have play doctor kits available and encourage them to heal dolls, stuffed animals, and each other! (You can also do this by role-playing scripture passages where people are healed.) Although this isn't a direct way of doing service, it allows preschoolers to play in ways that promote service, ways that will help them gain the skills needed to serve as they become older.

Ideas for 6- to 9-Year-olds

• **Assemble first-aid kits for those who may not be able to afford over-the-counter medications and other medical necessities.** Include common items such as: acetaminophen (since aspirin isn't recommended for children), bandages, antiseptic solution (such as hydrogen peroxide), antiseptic cream (such as bacitracin), hydrocortisone cream (for bites and stings), soap, thermometer, syrup of ipecac, and cotton-tipped swabs.

• **Have children put sunscreen on toddlers and preschoolers in your church before they go out on warm, sunny days.**

• **Talk about 2 Kings 20:1-11 and how King Hezekiah got very sick and then got well.** When children are sick in your class, create get-well packets. Ask each child to draw a picture for the sick person and add things they think would help the child feel better, such as stickers, pages cut out of a puzzle book (as long as you give them your permission to do that), coloring pages, and so on.

Ideas for 10- to 12-Year-olds

• **Study Isaiah 58:8-12.** Work with your pastor and worship committee on creating a service of healing, one that's either for everybody and talks about healing in general or a separate service for those who feel like they need healing. Encourage children to plan and take leadership roles in this service, using their unique gifts, talents, and skills.

• **Offer a pharmacy pick-up service for people who may not be able to easily get their prescriptions.**

• **Arrange for your children to receive training in CPR and the Heimlich maneuver.** Children who know these emergency procedures have used them on occasion and literally saved lives. Or invite someone from the American Red Cross to teach children the basics of first aid. Practice these techniques and talk about why learning these techniques is important for mission and service.

Helpful organizations

For the address, phone number, and web site of these organizations, see the Mission and Service Index starting on page 119.

• **Save the Children**—This organization sponsors a number of programs to help children who live in poverty throughout the world.

• **Sunshine Foundation**—This organization promotes hope for children who are seriously ill.

• Help •

Children naturally are curious and want to help, and the more we encourage these behaviors, the more likely children will continue to act in these ways as they grow and mature. Unfortunately, children often don't have the skills that match their helping enthusiasm and so it's easy for adults to take over and do things for them. However, that doesn't nurture children's long-term desire to help.

Hebrews 6:9-12 talks about this eagerness to help. Encourage and support children's need to help and their pride in doing so since these are key ingredients in creating lifelong helpers.

Ideas for 3- to 5-Year-olds

• **Whenever your congregation does a service or mission project, find a way for preschoolers to help.** Preschoolers can carry trowels for adults during planting service projects. They can be in charge of the snacks for painting project breaks. Always have adequate supervision for preschoolers and expect them to contribute only a little. But by exposing them to service projects and giving them small, easy tasks that they can do, their sense of achievement is strengthened.

• **Talk about 3 John 5-8 and how the Bible says we should help people.** When you're together, create helping buddies who help one another clean up the materials after craft projects and who walk together when you go to another room or go outside.

• **Call your local zoo to find out about an animal adoption program.** Your class can help an animal by creating a koala club, for example. Preschoolers can read books about koalas, visit the koala, and raise pennies and nickels to help the koala.

Ideas for 6- to 9-Year-olds

• **Read Ecclesiastes 4:9-12 to the children.** Discuss the fact that when everyone pitches in to help, it makes a bigger difference than when one person does something alone. Illustrate this point by asking for only one volunteer when your room is messy after a project. Ask that one person to do the cleanup while everyone else watches. After a few minutes, stop the child (and also be able to console the child if the child becomes frustrated and upset) and have everyone help. Afterward talk about why it's better when we all do our part to help.

• **Help a local community beach by having a beach cleanup day.** Beaches often are littered with trash, and it's easy for children to see their progress on a beach, compared to picking up trash along a highway where there can be high weeds.

• **Create a sock-it-away fund-raiser.** Ask children to each bring in one clean sock (which will later be returned) with loose change in it to help the charity that the group has chosen.

Ideas for 10- to 12-Year-olds

• **Ask someone to read aloud 1 Thessalonians 5:12-18.** Find out when your community, child-care centers, or schools have fairs or carnivals and offer to help. Children can sell raffle tickets, run a booth, decorate children's faces with nontoxic face paint, and publicize the event. Fairs require a lot of people power, and children can be of great help.

• **Contact a local service agency to wrap presents that have been purchased for families in need.** Often service agencies collect items unwrapped and then later need them wrapped. Children can help with the wrapping.

• **Set up a Halloween help for the homeless.** In addition to trick-or-treating, encourage children to also ask for a can of food to give to the homeless. After the trick-or-treating, have a Halloween party for children to bring all the food collected and to celebrate.

• **Help staff a food pantry.** Children can place cans on shelves and help sort food.

Helpful organizations

For the address, phone number, and web site of these organizations, see the Mission and Service Index starting on page 119.

• **Habitat for Humanity**—By building and repairing homes throughout the United States and around the world, this organization is doing essential work in providing housing for many people who can't afford it.

• **Points of Light Foundation**—This national organization has key information on service and mission on a national and local level.

▪ Learn ▪

"Learn to do right. See that justice is done—help those who are oppressed, give orphans their rights, and defend widows," says Isaiah 1:17 (TEV). An essential part of service and mission is *learning.* Not only is it important for children to learn to take responsibility and do their part, it's also essential that they learn and grow in the midst of doing service.

One of the growing movements within the service area is the field of service-learning. Organizations that do service-learning contend that combining service and learning produces a greater impact than when service and learning are done separately. Approaching service and mission from a service-learning perspective means that you emphasize essential learning, such as teaching children how to find meaning and purpose in their acts of caring and service and how to be active, informed citizens. But what's more important about service-learning is that it's about finding the unique learnings that come out of the individual service and mission projects that you do.

Ideas for 3- to 5-year-olds

- **Emphasize how children can learn to make others happy.** As a group learn a few songs to sing to parents, a youth group, or at a quilter's circle at your church. Afterward talk about how when you learn something new and share it with others, that brings people joy.
- **Help children learn about caring for each other.** Whenever someone is absent from your group or class, make a class "We missed you" card. (However, if you have a lot of children with irregular attendance who live in different locations because of separated or divorced parents, make "Get well" cards to send to classmates who are sick or hospitalized instead.) You write the words on the cards and have children sign their names and draw a picture if they wish. Mail them the next day. (Check with your church office since some churches have a budget for sending greeting cards.)

- **Simplify Philippians 4:9 for children so that they learn the message of this scripture:** "Do what you have learned" (TEV). Teach children the importance of cleaning up and putting things away after they're finished. Every time you do a craft, cooking project, or other activity that creates a mess, have children clean up and put things away afterward. Make this easy for children by having storage bins, drawers, and containers with pictures of the items that they hold. (For example, have a storage box with a picture of crayons on it, another box with a picture of construction paper on it, and another box with a picture of blocks on it.) As you clean up, sing a song together or talk about how you're doing what you've learned—that it's important to clean up after yourself.

Ideas for 6- to 9-Year-olds

• **Help children learn about a specific topic that you can make concrete, such as trash (where you emphasize the litter outside) or recycling (where you show children different recycling bins or visit a recycling center in your community).** Have children make posters to advocate for these causes, such as reminding people not to litter and encouraging people to recycle. Hang these posters around your congregation and community.

• **Talk about Titus 3:14:** "Our people must learn to spend their time doing good, in order to provide for real needs; they should not live useless lives" (TEV). Take your group to a children's cancer ward at a local hospital or visit an emergency child-care center. (Get permission from these places and from the parents of the children before you do this.) Ask children to pay attention to what they're seeing and to think of ideas for helping the children in need. Afterward, as you get started on one of the ideas, talk about how spending time in these places can help us learn about the needs people have.

• **As a group, learn about hospitality and the importance of serving others first.** Every time you have a snack, have one child distribute the napkins and cups (and any plates or utensils needed) while another child distributes the snack (serving everyone else first before serving her- or himself). An older child can pour the drinks. Each week, rotate the servers so that everyone gets the chance to serve in these different ways.

Ideas for 10- to 12-Year-olds

• **Discuss Proverbs 24:30-34.** Emphasize verse 32: "I looked at this, thought about it, and learned a lesson from it" (TEV). Although this scripture condemns the lazy action of another person, it's an important lesson for everyone to take action. Blaming does not get the work done. When you do a project as a group to help someone (such as painting the fence of a person who is homebound), talk about why it may be tempting to blame the person you're helping and why it's important to work through those feelings so that you can do your part to help.

● **Choose a specific country (or a specific missionary) to learn about as a group.** Gather research on what it's like to live in that country and the needs of the people who live there. Then find a way to serve that country or missionary. (Missionaries often enjoy letters and need specific items, which you can find out about.) Often a country will have a relief organization that can give you ideas on how you can help. War-torn countries typically have a number of organizations that accept donations, and newspapers and magazines often list these organizations.

● **Invite someone from the American Red Cross to teach children the basics of baby-sitting that are appropriate for ten- to twelve-year-olds to know.** As a group, offer a free child-care service one afternoon at your church to give parents some free time off and older children the chance to care and play with younger children in a service project. Remember to get adequate adult supervision for this project.

Helpful organizations

For the address, phone number, and web site of these organizations, see the Mission and Service Index starting on page 119.

● **National Youth Leadership Council**—This organization emphasizes the role of service-learning in doing service and mission projects.

● **United Methodist Children's Fund for Christian Mission**—An ideal way for children to learn about mission and service, this organization has packets that children's classes can use so that children can learn about and make contributions to a select group of mission projects of their choice.

• Mentor •

Scripture is filled with mentors. In 1 Samuel 3:1-21, you can read about the mentoring relationship between Eli and the boy Samuel. In 2 Kings 2:1-6, the scripture clearly spells out how Elijah was a mentor to Elisha. Mentors are role models who have close relationships with the person or people they're mentoring. Typically we think of adults being mentors for teenagers, yet everyone can be a mentor—even a young child.

Ideas for 3- to 5-Year-olds

• **Create preschool pals by matching up older preschoolers with younger preschoolers.** (Ideally you would have a five-year-old matched with a three-year-old.) Encourage the growth of these relationships by having one short activity during each meeting time so that these preschool pals can do something together. For example, preschool pals can build a tower. They can look at a book together. They can clean up a specific area of the room. What's important is that the two have some type of activity to do together where they can start forming a relationship.

• **Emphasize Proverbs 22:17-18 and the message of teaching others what you know.** Preschoolers can be mentors to infants in the nursery by becoming nursery helpers. Arrange for short periods of time for preschoolers to help out in the nursery. Preschoolers can get diapers for babies that need changing. They can play with babies and show picture books to babies. Supervise preschoolers closely in these interactions while encouraging them to be big helpers.

• **Match families of preschoolers with families of infants or families who are expecting a child.** It's easy for families who are expecting or who have infants to feel isolated, and creating family mentors can help encourage community. Plus preschoolers, particularly those who are only children or who happen to be the youngest in their families, can feel like a big brother or big sister to the young child in the other family.

Ideas for 6- to 9-Year-olds

• **Discuss Acts 5:29-32 and talk about how we obey God when we reach out to others.** Have members of your class become mentors for members of a younger class. (For example, second-graders can become mentors for members of a kindergarten class.) Arrange for the two classes to get together on a regular basis (such as monthly or semi-monthly) where the older class helps teach a lesson, gives a

puppet show, or sings a song with the younger children. During these class interactions, also create some one-to-one times so children can start to learn one another's names and get to know one another.

- **As children begin to learn to read, give them experience in reading aloud to toddlers and preschoolers.** Call children "book buddies" and encourage them to find a book to practice and master before reading it aloud to a group of younger children. Allow each child the experience of reading aloud.

- **Put children in charge of playing games with preschool-age children in your church.** Encourage them to choose games that three- to five-year-olds enjoy playing, such as hide and seek and tag. Talk about the important role children have in planning and playing these games with younger children.

Ideas for 10- to 12-Year-olds

- **Near Halloween, have ten- to twelve-year-olds help younger children carve pumpkins under the supervision of an adult.** Children also can roast pumpkin seeds for a snack. Ask children to find out interesting information about the children they're helping to encourage more interaction.

- **Study Hebrews 11 and talk about the mentors of faith, such as Abraham and Moses.** Discuss how children can be mentors for young children by being tutors. While school subjects are common areas for tutoring, other areas can be also, such as teaching children how to play chess or how to yo-yo. Ask children what they'd like to teach younger children to do. They often have many ideas.

- **Create church partners for ten- to twelve-year-olds and children who are slightly younger than they are.** Each month design two questions for children to ask their partners (such as their birth date, favorite dessert, favorite game, easiest school subject, etc.). Since some children feel shy about getting to know children of other ages or from other schools, this will provide the partners with a way to start the conversation. Encourage church partners to seek each other out during worship services and other church functions.

Helpful organizations

For the address, phone number, and web site of these organizations, see the Mission and Service Index starting on page 119.

- **Big Brothers/Big Sisters of America**—One of the most well-known mentoring programs, this organization pairs adult volunteers with children and youth who benefit from the extra attention of a caring adult.

- **One Plus One**—This organization is a clearinghouse of information on the topic of mentoring.

• Organize •

Great power is there when children come together and organize service projects. In many ways, that's how Jesus' ministry started and continued throughout his time on earth. Jesus didn't do the work alone, he called twelve disciples. Moreover, reaching out to a variety of people was an important part of organizing his work (John 1:35-51).

While adults can assist children, it's essential that children have some of the leadership responsibility in planning, decision making, organizing, and implementing the work of service and mission. Even preschoolers can make simple decisions and feel like they have valued input. By bringing children together, we can show them that while it's true that one person can make a difference, when you organize a group, the group can make an even bigger difference—and more quickly.

Ideas for 3- to 5-Year-olds

● **When your congregation has a service project, have preschoolers be the organizers and announcers of the schedule.** (An adult needs to keep track of this, but the preschoolers can do the announcing.) For example, preschoolers can announce snack times, break times, lunch times, and the arrival of supplies.

● **Have preschoolers sort and organize items for a recycling project or donation collection.** (For example, preschoolers can sort shoes into one pile, coats into another pile, socks into another, and clothes into a separate pile during a clothing drive.)

● **Explain that Leviticus 8 talks about everyone coming together to celebrate an important event.** On teacher recognition Sunday at your church, have preschoolers present a flower, ribbon, or some other token to each teacher. Give preschoolers choices of what to present and have them decide as a group which item to give. Preschoolers can also decide if they want to sing a song or play instruments to celebrate the event. An adult can do all the talking, and the preschoolers can hand out the items. (If you don't have a teacher recognition Sunday, start one by working with the worship committee to designate a portion of a worship service at the end of the Christian education year for this purpose.) Discuss how recognizing the good work other people do is a part of serving others.

Ideas for 6- to 9-Year-olds

- **Talk about Isaiah 11:10-16 and its central message of how people who come together can make quick changes.** Create a "Ready, Set, Clean" team where every child knows her or his role in cleaning up the room or a service project. When roles are clarified from the start, progress can go quickly.

- **Have children help organize the system to stuff a church mailing or bulletin that includes several loose announcements.** Churches often have stuffing projects, and children can serve in this way periodically. The older children can design the system or process that the group will use to do the work.

- **Children can design and decorate a large donation box for church collection drives.** Providing a designated spot that everyone knows about can help organize a service project.

Ideas for 10- to 12-Year-olds

- **Have children organize a cemetery cleanup day for a nearby cemetery.** (Children usually find this setting an interesting place for a litter cleanup.) Make sure you find a cemetery that doesn't have regular cleanup maintenance, such as a small or rural cemetery.

- **Study Genesis 49, where Jacob gathers everyone together and shares his vision of the future for each person.** Although this passage has bad news in addition to good news, it also shows how essential it is to come together to discuss issues. Develop a "Service Central" where children come together on a regular basis (whether that be monthly or quarterly) to discuss service project ideas and ways they can organize a helping project.

- **Children can make maps with direction to an off-site congregation-wide service project.** You can find map programs on the computer or check out maps from your local library to create the maps. (Give children assistance, however, so that the maps are accurate. Some children photocopy maps and mark them up. Other children enjoy drawing maps based on actual maps.) Then have children create a distribution plan for their maps.

Helpful organizations

For the address, phone number, and web site of these organizations, see the Mission and Service Index starting on page 119.

- **Natural Guard**—This hands-on organization helps children identify and solve their local community's problems.

- **SERVEnet**—Find volunteer opportunities in your community through this organization.

• Partner •

Working together in partnerships is how the Amish can do barn raising and house building in short amounts of time. Individuals do their part and work with others who have different skills.

In Paul's letter to the Philippians, he mentions how grateful he is for the work others have done in partnership with him. "I thank my God for you every time I think of you; and every time I pray for you all, I pray with joy because of the way in which you have helped me in the work of the gospel from the very first day until now" (Philippians 1:3-5 TEV). When children partner with other children or adults, they can serve in ways that they would never be able to do alone.

Ideas for 3- to 5-Year-olds

• **Mention that Nehemiah 3:1-16 talks about how everybody has an important task to do and how a lot can get done when everybody does her or his part.** Create threesome partnerships where children each have a specific role in making a homemade card to give to someone in need. (Start out with white construction paper that has been cut and folded into the size of cards.) One child in each partnership can use rubber stamps to add stamp pictures. Another child can add stickers. Another child can color with markers. After they have made two cards, have them switch roles. Afterward, talk about how much was accomplished by working together.

• **Find out when someone in your congregation (who has a dog or cat) is going on vacation.** Ask if your preschool group can care for the pet on one day only (since it's too difficult for preschoolers to have responsibility for longer than that). As a group, visit the pet (but be careful not to overwhelm the animal). Have children change the water dish, provide food and treats (if appropriate), walk the pet (if it's a dog), and play with the pet. Talk about how we can all work together to care for an animal.

• **Partner with older children or teenagers in the fall to rake leaves.** Although preschoolers won't get a lot done, they can pick up individual leaves and put them into bags. They also can add a spirit of fun and play to the service project, which often lifts the spirits of the people doing the raking and bagging.

Ideas for 6- to 9-Year-olds

• **Partner with the youth choir to create a multi-age young person's choir to sing during worship on a specific Sunday.** (The choir could be for young people in kindergarten to twelfth grade.) Work on ways to get young people to mingle with one another while they learn songs.

Teaching Kids to Care & Share

- **In Philemon 17, Paul encourages Philemon to think of him as a partner.** As a group, brainstorm ideas of service projects children would like to see done but feel they need adult help with. (For example, children may decide that your church needs a sandbox for toddlers and preschoolers.) Once children have chosen a service project, create a partnership with adults in your congregation who can help them make their service project become a reality.

- **Organize a congregation-wide vegetable swap during harvest season if you have a lot of members who have vegetable gardens.** (People who grow vegetables often have more than they can use.) Children can help man the tables while people set out their vegetables and either swap or give them away. (Publicize that this event is for everyone in the congregation, not just those who have gardens, since gardeners often are happy to share their extras with those without gardens.)

Ideas for 10- to 12-Year-olds

- **Get in touch with a soup kitchen and make a commitment for your group to serve a meal on a regular basis (whether twice a year or four times a year).** Making a commitment is an important partnership not only for your children to serve but also for the soup kitchen so the workers know of volunteers they can depend on.

- **Form a partnership with a group of children who are different from your children.** For example, if you have a number of children with physical disabilities, link up with a group with mental disabilities. Periodically visit the group you're partnering with and do service projects together. For example, together the children can collect phone books for recycling or they can learn songs to sing to young children.

- **Study 1 Corinthians 3:5-9.** Discuss verse 9 in detail: "For we are partners working together for God, and you are God's field. You are also God's building" (TEV). Talk about what this means in terms of partnerships and service. Partner with a greenhouse or agricultural extension office that can provide ivy and other cuttings for children to plant and grow. The plants can be used as a fund-raiser or can be given to people who need some cheer.

Helpful organizations

For the address, phone number, and web site of these organizations, see the Mission and Service Index starting on page 119.

- **Second Harvest**—This network of national food banks distributes food to shelters, senior citizen centers, and soup kitchens.

- **United Way of America**—The Young America Cares program of the United Way of America has many ideas on how your group can partner with them in volunteer efforts.

• Plant •

The parable of the sower in Matthew 13:1-9 is one of the most familiar stories in scripture about planting. It is a story rich with metaphor, telling what happens when seed falls among thorn bushes, when seed falls on the path and gets eaten by birds, when seed falls onto rocky soil, and when seed falls into good soil. It's one of the few parables that can easily be illustrated and made concrete for children by actually taking them outdoors and showing them what happens when you sow seeds in these ways.

Planting is another way that children can serve others. Plants can be fruits and vegetables that provide food for others. Plants can be flowers that add cheer to people's lives. Plants can include trees, shrubs, grass, and more. Planting is a way that children can get their hands into God's soil and make a difference in a hands-on way.

Ideas for 3- to 5-Year-olds

• **Talk about Ecclesiastes 3:2, which says that there is a time for planting and a time for harvesting.** As a group, plant a vegetable that you can easily harvest, such as tomatoes. (Tomato plants can grow indoors when they have adequate light and water.) As the vegetables are growing, periodically check on the plants so that children can see the progress. After the plants are harvested, have the children sell them in a church fund-raiser. Adults usually can't resist buying a tomato from a three-, four-, or five-year-old.

• **Make soup-can flower baskets.** (Take the labels off of the soup cans—or vegetable or fruit cans—and ask a handy adult to drill two holes in the can near the top so you can create a pipe-cleaner handle for this aluminum-can basket.) Have children choose the color of pipe cleaner they want to use for a handle and then decorate the cans with stickers and markers. With the children's help, transplant a marigold or some other flower into the can to make a flower basket. Make these for Mother's Day, Grandparent's Day, or to give to another group of people whom you wish to serve.

• **Inquire about getting a donation of several small house plants in plastic pots (or buy them inexpensively at a greenhouse or discount store).** Have children decorate the plastic pots with cheery stickers. As a group, visit a nursing home or long-term care facility for children and give plants to individuals.

Ideas for 6- to 9-Year-olds

• **Get permission to plant pumpkins on your church property or find someone in your congregation who is willing to donate a large portion of garden space so that each child can grow a pumpkin as well as have extras to give away.** Plant the seeds together as a group. Once the pumpkins appear (and are green), help each child carve her or his name with a soft knife (so that you penetrate only the skin of the pumpkin, not the actual vegetable) in a pumpkin of her or his choosing. Periodically check the progress. As the pumpkins grow, so will the names carved into the skin. At harvesttime, talk about how God likes it when we plant good food to grow and how God also likes it when we grow. Give away the extra pumpkins to families with young children in your church.

- **Read aloud Jeremiah 29:5:** "Build houses and settle down. Plant gardens and eat what you grow in them" (TEV). Ask every child to name her or his favorite fruit and favorite vegetable. Take children to a nearby farmer's market or vegetable stand. Buy a treat for children to eat. As a group, thank God for the good food that is planted to make us strong. Pray for those who don't have access to fresh fruits and vegetables. Talk about how prayer is another form of service and mission.

- **Plant bulbs in the fall for your church and members of your church who are bedridden or homebound.** Have adult volunteers on hand to assist with digging holes. In the spring, take a tour with your group to see the results of your planting.

Ideas for 10- to 12-Year-olds

- **Find a boulevard, run-down parkway, or some other community place (get permission from the appropriate community office or agency first) to commit to beautifying the area over the long term.** Look for these places in residential and commercial areas of your community. Have children work with an adult who understands flower landscaping so that the children can plan how to design the area. Plant the area and occasionally weed it to ensure that it's growing well. Some groups take this project on over a number of years and gradually expand it with the hopes of turning around an area that was once void of plants and beauty.

- **Create a lawn-care service for people in your community who have difficulty caring for their own lawns or who can't afford to pay for a lawn service.** Team up with some older teenagers and adults who can assist with driving and doing some of the more technical work. Ten- to twelve-year-old children can mow lawns (although they usually need an adult to help with starting the mower and emptying the bag). Children also can push the fertilizer spreaders, although they may need some assistance in filling the spreader and adjusting it so that the proper amount of fertilizer is distributed.

- **Give each child one seed from a packet of seeds.** Ask one of the children to read aloud the parable of the mustard seed in Mark 4:30-32. Talk about the power that a single seed has. Have children plant seeds (planting enough for four to six plants in order to ensure that at least one or two plants grow) in small containers. Have children care for the seeds. When the plants grow, have children give them to younger children in your church.

Helpful organizations

For the address, phone number, and web site of these organizations, see the Mission and Service Index starting on page 119.

- **America the Beautiful Fund**—This organization has free seed packets for planting when you send a request with an SASE.

- **National Arbor Day Foundation**—Receive free seedlings and information about planting trees through this organization.

▪ Play ▪

Creating service projects that center around play is a great way for children to do what comes naturally to them while also bringing cheer to other children. Romans 15:30-33 emphasizes that we should bring joy to others.

Although many adults think playing isn't a form of service, it's actually the ideal form of service for children. For children, play is not only a source of learning, it's also a source of great joy. For children to be who they are, children must play. Playing with children who have understimulating environments or who live in difficult circumstances is a great way to serve these children. When children play, they feel good about themselves and they build essential relationships.

Ideas for 3- to 5-Year-olds

• **Have your preschoolers visit the toddlers and play with them during the toddlers' self-directed time.** Encourage preschoolers to join in on the toddlers' play but not to take over the play.

• **Take preschoolers to an animal shelter to play with the animals.** Get permission from parents and from the animal shelter ahead of time so that the shelter staff can determine the best animals for this age group to play with.

• **Talk about John 15:11-17 and how we can have fun by playing together and caring for each other.** Let preschoolers take turns choosing the game they love to play most as a way of serving your group.

Ideas for 6- to 9-Year-olds

• **If you have small classes of children, partner with a small church to arrange for kickball games, T-ball games, and other group sports that you otherwise wouldn't be able to do alone.** Encourage children to form teams that have children from both churches to help build relationships between children.

• **Discuss Psalm 126 and how it emphasizes laughing and singing for joy.** See if your local hospital has a rolling toy cart that has toys, games, and fun activities for children who are bedridden. If the hospital doesn't, make this a service project. If the hospital does, have your group volunteer to play with the children.

• **Have this age group play simple musical instruments with the preschoolers in your church.** Sand blocks, tambourines, sticks, drums, and cymbals are always a big hit with young children. They'll enjoy making music together.

Ideas for 10- to 12-Year-olds

• **Study Galatians 5:22-23.** Talk about how creating service projects that emphasize play can build each of the characteristics mentioned in this scripture. When your group notices the younger children in your church playing outside or playing on your church playground, make it a time of service. Have your group play with the younger children, helping them get into swings, pushing them on swings, building sand castles with them, going down the slide with them, and so on. Young children love the attention of older children.

• **Create a toy box service project where you create "imagination toy chests" for low-income preschools.** Include dress-up clothes, play telephones, costumes, and other items that children can use for their imaginary play.

• **Have children bring their favorite card games and board games to a nursing home or senior residential center to play games with those who live there.**

Helpful organizations

For the address, phone number, and web site of these organizations, see the Mission and Service Index starting on page 119.

• **Toys for Tots**—This organization collects children's toys to distribute to children in need.

• **USA Toy Library Association**—By facilitating the development of toy lending libraries and other programs, this organization promotes the importance of play for children.

• Reach Out •

Many scripture passages point out the importance of reaching out to others, especially to those in need. Job 29:11-17 mentions people who are poor, orphaned, widowed, blind, lame, victims of crime, and strangers in trouble. Our communities and our country are filled with people children can reach out to and serve.

Ideas for 3- to 5-Year-olds

• **Point out that Leviticus 25:35-38 says we should reach out and care for others, especially those who don't have as much as we have.** Encourage preschoolers to buy an extra toy at Christmastime for a child who can't afford one. Arrange to give these toys to a social service agency in your community that needs new toys for the children it serves.

• **Take flowers to parents after they send their freshmen off to college in the fall.** Having a group of preschoolers visit with a bouquet of flowers often can cheer up parents who are feeling the effects of the empty nest for the first time.

• **Call a battered women's shelter or homeless shelter and say your preschoolers want to celebrate a birthday of someone in their care.** Ask the shelter to suggest a day and time and who the party will be for. As a group, bake a cake and make birthday cards for each child to give. Then on the day, have a birthday party at the shelter.

Ideas for 6- to 9-Year-olds

• **Have children bring tapered candles to parents of newborns who are at the hospital right after giving birth.** Children can suggest the parents have a candlelight dinner in the room to celebrate the arrival of their new family member. Check with hospital personnel first to make sure you're not violating any safety regulations. If the hospital won't allow candles, children can still bring dinner or a batch of cookies.

• **When your church has a mission offering, have children make red construction-paper hearts for each member of the congregation.** On each heart, have children write "Care and Give." When the mission offering is announced during worship, have children distribute the hearts to each person in the congregation. Ask an older child to make an announcement about the heart reminders for this mission offering.

- **Talk about Acts 21:17-26 and how it stresses the importance of reaching out to keep people up to date.** As children do service projects, have them also give reports and updates to your church's governing board or governing committee. It's a service for your church when children keep adults informed about the progress of their service projects.

Ideas for 10- to 12-Year-olds

- **Study Ephesians 4:11-16.** Discuss how apostles, prophets, evangelists, teachers, and pastors reach out to other people. Then talk about the unique differences between the different roles these people have. On one Sunday, arrange for each child to be an assistant for a different teacher in your church. Children can serve other children and a teacher by doing this.
- **Find out the names of college students in your congregation.** Contact their families to learn when final exams occur. Then organize a cookie-baking service project to send each student a dozen cookies to receive at the beginning of final exams. (If your congregation has a lot of college students, you might want to make this a congregation-wide service project or at least a partnership with a youth group.) Include good-luck greetings with the cookies.
- **Make heart-shaped cookies for Valentine's Day and deliver them to people who are widowed or homebound in your congregation.**

Helpful organizations

For the address, phone number, and web site of these organizations, see the Mission and Service Index starting on page 119.
- **Community Partnerships with Youth, Inc.**—This organization promotes active citizenship through youth and adult community partnerships, creating ways to reach out to each other and connect.
- **National Council on the Aging**—This organization aims to improve the lives of the elderly.

▪ Read ▪

One of the major movements in this country is to eliminate illiteracy and to bring reading materials to everyone—children and adults alike. For many people education is a ticket to creating a better life and a better world, and it's impossible to get an education without knowing how to read.

Even in Jesus' teaching, he often made his point by asking, "Haven't you ever read what the Scriptures say?" (Matthew 21:42) or "Have you never read what David did?" (Matthew 12:3) or "Haven't you read?" (Matthew 19:4). Reading is the first step to change. We read, we learn, we act in new ways. And children can create many service and mission projects to promote reading.

Ideas for All Children

● **Make bookmarks.**
Preschoolers can decorate bookmarks with stickers and rubber stamps. Older children can make more elaborate bookmarks that look like stained-glass windows or have patterns cut out in them. Each child can make a bookmark to place in a book given to a child who lives in a shelter or to children who live in foster care.

● **Children of all ages can collect books for book drives, and it's actually better when you have children of many different ages involved to attract a lot of different reading levels and themes.** From board books for infants and toddlers to chapter books for older children, book drives are a great way to bring new reading material to a low-income child-care center or to families who can't afford to buy books.

● **Children can serve important roles at book fairs by manning booths, creating publicity flyers, talking about the books they've read, and so on.**

Ideas for 3- to 5-Year-olds

● **Give preschoolers pictures of animals and simple objects (or have board books with these items in them) and link up with toddlers in your congregation.** Have the preschoolers hold up the pictures one at a time and ask "What's this?" to the toddlers. You can do this as a group activity or by making small groups with the assistance of an adult. Preschoolers think it's amazing how quickly toddlers can learn how to identify animals, things, and people.

● **Talk about how Ezra read aloud to the people in Nehemiah 8:1-3, just like you read aloud to preschoolers.** Bring in a bunch of age-appropriate books (if your room doesn't have a large number already) and give children time to look through books to find their absolute favorite. When they do find a favorite, have them take turns showing the group their favorite book. Although preschoolers can't read, they can show the pictures to the group and make up their own stories if they wish. Talk about how showing books to the group is a form of service.

● **Create "read-to-me group sessions" by bringing adults and preschoolers together so that preschoolers can crawl into the lap of an adult and the adult can read to the child.** (Match one preschooler with one adult, and do this in a group setting.) Although this may appear to be a service project for adults, often it's the preschoolers who are giving as much back since crawling into someone's lap and having close interactions are rare these days.

Ideas for 6- to 9-Year-olds

● **Have children play "guess the rhyme" with preschoolers.** Have the six- to nine-year-olds find a book of nursery rhymes and teach them how to make games out of rhymes. For example, "Humpty Dumpty sat on the wall. Humpty Dumpty had a great _____ ." Preschoolers love this guessing game, and older children will enjoy trying to stump younger children.

● **Match older, more experienced readers in your group with younger, less experienced readers.** Have the less experienced readers read aloud to their more experienced reader buddies. Teach the more experienced reader to listen, not jump in to correct, and gently support and encourage the blossoming reader.

● **Talk about how Jeremiah 36:1-10 tells about reading aloud to people and how reading helps us learn how to act as Christians.** Each week, put a different child in charge of the reading for the class.

The child gets to choose two books (from a collection that you've created) and shares them with the class (either through reading or by talking about the pictures).

Ideas for 10- to 12-Year-olds

- **Have children participate in a read-a-thon (like a walk-a-thon, except with reading books).** Have them get sponsors and set individual goals to raise money for an important cause by reading.
- **Encourage children to write their own books or stories to sell for a fund-raiser.** (Some children enjoy writing and illustrating their own books.) Find some adults in your congregation who work with writing (such as writers, public relations people, editors, journalists, and so on) to help mentor in this project.
- **Study Acts 15:22-35.** Talk about the power of writing and reading. Have children analyze the themes of books in their church, school, or community library. Do they represent the diversity and values they have? For example, children could decide that there aren't enough books about people of a certain race, from a certain country or culture, of girls who are successful, or of boys who are caring. Then they could seek the help of book lovers in the community to assist them in donating these books to that library. Or children could even create a book drive to start a library in a church that doesn't have a library or in a rural area that doesn't have a community library.

Helpful organizations

For the address, phone number, and web site of these organizations, see the Mission and Service Index starting on page 119.

- **Lutheran Braille Workers Inc.**—This organization provides Braille and large-print Bibles and Christian reading materials to people with visual impairments.
- **Reading Is Fundamental**—Give the gift of books through this organization so that children who are homeless or at risk can learn to read.

• Record •

Because of situations ranging from blindness to illiteracy to just plain busyness, many people can be served by recordings that they can listen to or watch during their own time. Whether the stories are read from published books or created by the children, children enjoy doing recordings once they get over the initial embarrassment or suspicion about them.

Creating recordings as a service project is a way of remembering: remembering those who are forgotten, remembering important messages, remembering what's important. Second Timothy 1:3-7 talks about remembering, and making recordings that remind people how much they mean to each other is a service we all benefit from.

Ideas for 3- to 5-Year-olds

• **Make audiotapes and/or videotapes of preschoolers singing songs or doing a short program.** Either sell the tapes as a fund-raiser for a good cause or distribute the tapes to grandparents and extended family members who live far away. (Although you should be aware that parents and other people in your church may be highly interested in these tapes.)

• **Have preschoolers talk, sing, and give messages that you record and send to another preschooler who has been hospitalized or is away visiting a parent in another state for a number of months, or to a significant adult in your church (such as a pastor, youth leader, or organist) who may be sick.**

• **Teach preschoolers Proverbs 17:17a:** "Friends always show their love" (TEV). Talk about how we show our love by serving others and doing good things for them. One way the group can do something worthwhile is by collecting audio music tapes, books on tape, and videotapes of materials that preschoolers enjoy. Often families have outgrown these and they're happy to give them away when they no longer use them. Or people can donate recordings that they've made or purchased. Find a child-care center, social-service agency, hospital, or other place (like a Ronald McDonald house) that would enjoy receiving this donation.

Ideas for 6- to 9-Year-olds

• **Read aloud Hebrews 13:21.** Talk about how serving others is a way "to do [God's] will" (TEV). Have children record tapes of preschool songs that the preschoolers are learning so that each preschooler can have a tape to bring home and listen to while learning the song.

• **Make lullaby tapes for parents of newborns or to give as baby shower gifts.** Children can learn and sing these songs.

• **Visit a nature center and make recordings of the birds and nature sounds.** Give these to charities that help children who live in cities and those who rarely get the chance to visit nature. Or give them to adults who are bedridden and rarely see the out-of-doors.

• **Link up with children at another church (or another organization) and create humorous recordings as a way to bring laughter to other children.** Children can make funny noises and unusual sound effects (which are often a big hit) or they can sing in funny ways or tell funny, appropriate jokes. Talk about how giving the gift of laughter is an important part of service.

Ideas for 10- to 12-Year-olds

• **Talk about how Numbers 1:20-46 emphasizes the history they've recorded.** Although this was not done through electronic means, the recording was a way for a lot of people to have access to information and also for many generations to have access to it. Have children create family history recordings by calling up different members of their family (grandparents, aunts, uncles, cousins, and so on) to hear about their favorite family memory. Some children can record these on a tape recorder (if they have access to that) or they can write down the memories and put them together in a book. Either way, they can give a copy of the audio tape or the book by making copies (with the help of an adult) as a way to serve and to preserve their family histories.

• **Have children read scripture stories (or other stories you deem suitable) to give to people who are in prison or people who are blind.** Or check with a prison ministry to see if your group can donate children's books, tape recorders, and audio tapes for prisoners who are parents to record books on tape for their children.

• **Have the more technologically interested children record the sermons and or worship services of your congregation to give to people recovering from surgery or people who are homebound or bedridden.** If this service already exists, children can deliver the tapes and visit with the recipients.

• **Have children record their favorite religious Christmas carols.** Make copies and distribute them to people who are homebound and bedridden. Sell additional copies to families and friends and use the money to give to a worthy cause.

• **Interview long-term members about memories of your church and events that happened long ago.** (For example, a member may know that the cross hanging in your church sanctuary was created by finding two discarded railroad ties and was erected by the youth group in 1967.) Make a booklet of these stories and distribute them to all who attend your church.

Helpful organizations

For the address, phone number, and web site of these organizations, see the Mission and Service Index starting on page 119.

• **Prison Fellowship**—Get in touch with and serve people who are in prison through this organization.

• **Recording for the Blind and Dyslexic**—This organization provides recordings for people with visual impairments.

• Recycle •

Through recycling, children can serve in ways that help not only the environment but also each other. By using things wisely, reusing them whenever possible, and recycling, we can create a more livable earth that's better for everyone.

Psalm 8 clearly emphasizes the essential role we have in caring for the earth, which includes recycling. Verses 6-8 in particular point out that we have the rule of leading and caring for creation. "You appointed them rulers over everything you made; you placed them over all creation: sheep and cattle, and the wild animals too; the birds and the fish and the creatures in the seas" (Psalm 8:6-8 TEV). By recycling, we create an environment that helps people and animals thrive.

Ideas for 3- to 5-Year-olds

• **Talk about Proverbs 3:19-20, emphasizing how God created the earth, and note that recycling is one way to take care of it.** In your classroom, create recycling bins: one for paper, one for cans, and one for plastic. (Find out the categories your community uses for recycling. Some communities for example, want magazines, newspaper, and other paper separated from one another. Other communities allow all paper to be mixed.) Teach children the differences between these recycling bins and have them use them whenever you're together.

• **In your classroom, use washable napkins made from fabric and washcloths to clean children's faces instead of paper napkins and paper towels.** Each week keep a running tally of how many washcloths and cloth napkins were used. At the end of the year, tally up the number and show children how much garbage they didn't create by using cloth washcloths and napkins. Emphasize how recycling also involves making good choices about the items we use. Once children understand this concept, volunteer as a group to handle all the cloth napkins for a church dinner or banquet. Children can place a napkin at each place setting before the dinner and can collect them and place them into a large bag for washing afterward.

• **Create a recycling bin fund-raiser.** First determine the kinds of items people tend to use a lot—for example, a lot of people drink beverages out of a can, while others tend to favor plastic bottles. Find out which items your community recycles, then set up bins in a prominent place in your church after you get permission. Have preschoolers keep tabs on the amount of material being collected and then determine how to distribute the money after the items have been recycled.

Ideas for 6- to 9-Year-olds

● **Set up a compost box on your church's property and encourage everyone to use it.** Those who mow the lawn can place grass clippings in it. People who use your church kitchen can add discarded food. After the compost is complete, as a group project use the compost to plant a small flower or vegetable garden.

● **Talk about how an important part of recycling is reusing things.** Encourage children to bring four or five toys that they no longer use to trade in a toy swap. (Get permission from parents before you do this.) Swapping toys is a great way for children to find new treasures and give away what they no longer use.

● **Read aloud Psalm 104:5-14.** Talk about how God did all these good things for the earth and we can do good things too by recycling and taking care of the earth. As a group, volunteer to help out at a recycling center. (First call to find out how the center can use the service of children.) Not only is this a good service project but it also gives children first-hand knowledge about the importance of recycling.

Ideas for 10- to 12-Year-olds

● **Offer the service of collecting live Christmas trees after the Christmas season.** With the help of adults, trim off the branches and save them to use for bush and shrub mulch in the spring. Chop the tree trunk into firewood to give away for free.

● **Study 1 Corinthians 3:5-9.** Emphasize verse 5*b*, "Each one of us does the work which the Lord gave him to do" (TEV). Discuss how recycling is one way to be God's servant. Find out from gas stations or oil-changing businesses if they recycle their motor oil. Find out the cost that they charge. Then create a flyer listing the places that offer this service and publicize it to people in your church.

● **Decorate recycling bins and place them in the kitchen, youth group room, or other places in your church where a lot of waste gathers.** Publicize these recycling bins to everyone. As a group, be in charge of taking the items to be recycled to the recycling center or to the recycling containers in your neighborhood or community.

Helpful organizations

For the address, phone number, and web site of these organizations, see the Mission and Service Index starting on page 119.

● **Kids for a Clean Environment (Kids F.A.C.E.)**—An environmental action club for children, this organization has a newsletter that keeps those interested in environmental issues up to date.

● **St. Jude's Ranch for Children**—Children in this facility collect donated used holiday cards to create new ones, which are then sold to raise money for their organization.

· Repair ·

"Your people will rebuild what has long been in ruins, building again on the old foundations. You will be known as the people who rebuilt the walls, who restored the ruined houses" (Isaiah 58:12 TEV). Repairing and rebuilding are important ways to serve. We can repair roofs and fences. We can rebuild garages and sheds that are falling down.

Adults typically do a lot of repair and rebuilding service projects, yet children have an important contribution to make in these projects. Although a five-year-old cannot repair a roof, a preschooler can assist in the repair, handing workers another box of nails or other supplies when needed. In addition, teaching children the importance of repairing and rebuilding things, instead of just replacing items, is a good way for them to learn how to serve and be good stewards.

Ideas for All Children

• **Visit your church nursery or toddler room and have children hunt for puzzle pieces and make simple toy repairs, such as putting the clothes back on dolls.**
• **If your church has plants, teach children how to gently remove the dead leaves on the plant and clean up the dead leaves that have fallen to the ground or into the pot.** Place the dead leaves into your church compost. Talk about how cleaning up the plants is a way to serve the congregation by making it look like a welcoming, lively place.

Ideas for 3- to 5-Year-olds

• **Talk about Amos 9:11-15, which discusses the repair work that God does, and describe the repair work that we should also do.** Help children develop a spirit of noticing and telling others when something is broken. (Often preschoolers simply become upset when something breaks.) Create a repair box for broken items, and talk about how to find people who can repair those items. (Encourage those adults to interact with the children and repair the items in their presence rather than having items miraculously become repaired.) Talk about how children will grow into adults who can repair things and tell them they have an important role now of finding things that need to be repaired.
• **Invite preschoolers to participate in congregation-wide service projects, such as a painting project.** Preschoolers can be in charge of distributing the paint brushes to the workers. They can also assist by collecting rolls of masking tape after taping has been done before painting.
• **If there's a wall in your church that has a lot of cracks or dents or is in bad shape, talk about**

how preschoolers can repair the wall by creating pictures to cover up the broken places. Make posters, pictures, and banners to hang on the wall.

Ideas for 6- to 9-Year-olds

- **Create a rechargeable battery campaign by collecting rechargeable batteries and rechargeable units to give to low-income families.** Batteries are expensive, and rechargeable batteries cost more than alkaline batteries. Yet alkaline batteries don't last as long, and they create more harm to the environment.

- **Talk about Nehemiah 3, where people rebuild the wall of Jerusalem.** Point out that like the wall of Jerusalem, things break, wear out, and need repair. Explain that one way children can keep the church running smoothly is by serving in a way that helps those who attend. If your church has pencil pews, have the children sharpen these pencils and place them back into the pews.

- **Visit a pediatric hospital ward or a pediatric medical clinic to make a list of the toys and books that need to be repaired.** Make a list of the items needed to repair the toys and books, including the names of adults who might help with specific repairs. Repair the items.

Ideas for 10- to 12-Year-olds

- **Halfway through the school year, set up a school repair time for children in kindergarten through third grade to bring in their notebooks, folders, and other school supplies that need repairing.** (A lot of these items start falling apart by this time, and children often are asking for them to be replaced.) Do repairs in ways that are artistic, such as creating designs on the masking tape to repair pocket folders.

- **Form a partnership with adults to work on repair projects for people who have difficulty with daily life tasks, such as people with Alzheimer's or with physical or mental disabilities.** Children can accompany adults to repair a car, washing machine, or dryer.

- **Read 1 Kings 18:30-39.** Talk about repairing the altar and how repairing is an important way to serve. Have children serve in the preparation of a church dinner. They can refill ketchup and mustard bottles and salt and pepper shakers. They can also pour salad dressing into serving bottles and so on. Talk about how these acts of service help people feel special when they come to eat.

Helpful organizations

For the address, phone number, and web site of these organizations, see the Mission and Service Index starting on page 119.

- **Alzheimer's Association**—People suffering from Alzheimer's disease are supported through this organization.

- **Federation for Children with Special Needs**—This organization works with children who have a variety of physical, mental, and emotional impairments.

• Respond •

Teaching children to become aware of what's happening around them and throughout the world is a way for them to learn the needs of people who may not request help outright. For example, when floods, tornadoes, and storms hit, children can respond and serve. When wars break out, children can do their part by responding to the situation.

Micah 4:1-4 talks about serving in ways that will bring peace to all people. By responding to people in need, children are bringing peace—not only to the people they're serving but also to the world in general.

Ideas for 3- to 5-Year-olds

• **When you hear about a family or a number of families losing their houses in a storm or to a natural disaster, have children collect toys.** Talk about how the children lost all their toys and how you can serve them by collecting new toys for them. Encourage preschoolers to select and give toys they would really like to have.

• **Talk about how Psalm 34:13-14 says we should do good things and explain that we can do good things by helping others.** Find out when someone in your church (someone who has been hospitalized, living in a different place during the winter months, or otherwise away for a period of time) is returning to church. Have the children greet the person to welcome her or him back by putting a sticker on the person (so the person is covered with stickers) to say how glad they are to see the person again.

• **Find out from a soup kitchen or homeless shelter if you can bring a large container of soup made by the preschoolers.** Make the soup by having all the ingredients cut up beforehand and then inviting different children to add different ingredients to the soup kettle. (Be careful about cooking safety.) As a group take the kettle to the soup kitchen or homeless shelter.

Ideas for 6- to 9-Year-olds

• **Create a church escort service.** Have children pair up with people who use walkers or canes. Children can carry their purses, bulletins, or Bibles, and help them get things they'd like, such as a glass of water. Children in wheelchairs can carry items in their laps.

The Actions of Mission and Service

- **People who volunteer in your nursery often enjoy the assistance of children to visit periodically and entertain babies.** Have children bring bubble solution and blow bubbles for the babies, which often makes them smile and giggle.
- **Create snack packs for children living in homeless shelters.** Include snacks that don't require refrigeration or won't spoil easily, such as nuts, raisins, cookies, crackers, boxed juice, apples, oranges, and pretzels.
- **Study Mark 16:15:** "Go into all the world and preach the good news to all creation" (NIV). In addition to telling the good news, we can act on the good news by responding to the needs around us. Not only do people have needs but so do organizations. Inquire about helping with a children's fund-raiser that's already in progress. Often the coordinators of these events are happy to receive extra help from children. Or find out which social service agency in your community could benefit from your children's help.

Ideas for 10- to 12-Year-olds

- **Study the newspaper and look for articles that give ideas for service projects.** For example, a story about a sick boy awaiting a kidney transplant can inspire children to help raise money for the cause.
- **Read 1 Peter 4:10.** Have children discuss which talents they have and how they can use their talents in order to respond to needs and serve others. For example, children could tutor younger children in reading or teach children in the hospital how to blow different bubbles with bubble gum.
- **Check with a nursing home or long-term residential facility to see if your group can come and take people in wheelchairs on walks.** Older children enjoy pushing people in wheelchairs, especially after learning how to push them at a good, even speed. (Children can create wheelchair buddies and learn how to push together or you might want to have some children work with an adult. Children in your group who are in wheelchairs can play wheelchair games with adults in wheelchairs.)
- **Help children role-play what it might be like to live through a disaster, such as an earthquake, tornado, or hurricane.** Collect information about these. Make a list of needed items. Choose some of these items and create a collection for them.

Helpful organizations

For the address, phone number, and web site of these organizations, see the Mission and Service Index starting on page 119.

- **American Red Cross**—By providing food, shelter, medical assistance, and other necessities, this organization helps those who live in places that have been hit by disaster.
- **Direct Relief International**—This organization provides medical assistance to people throughout the world who live in areas that are facing emergencies.

▪ Shop ▪

Acts 4:34-35 tells us to do good things with our money. Usually with service projects we encourage children to give money but then they don't see what happens with the money. You can create two-part service projects by having children raise money (or give their own money) and then use the money in ways that help others.

Ideas for 3- to 5-Year-olds

● **Talk about Genesis 42:2-10, which emphasizes buying food.** Have preschoolers buy pizzas and have a pizza party with your church's youth group. Most teenagers love pizza, and preschoolers will enjoy spending time with older kids who will respond enthusiastically to their gift.

● **Take preschoolers shopping for light items that they can carry, such as tissue boxes, toilet paper, paper towels, cotton balls, and so on.** Preschoolers can purchase paper products for people who are homebound or bedridden or for people who live in nursing homes. For example, preschoolers can take a box of tissues and a small bouquet of flowers to individuals who live in a senior residential home.

● **When teenagers and adults in your congregation do service projects, have preschoolers purchase beverages that they can serve to the workers.** In hot and warm weather, purchase iced tea and lemonade. In cold weather, purchase hot chocolate, tea, and coffee.

Ideas for 6- to 9-Year-olds

● **Make baby chicks out of yellow pom-poms, wiggly eyes, and felt.** Find out from Heifer Project International how much money children need to raise to give a flock of chicks to a family who needs them. Then determine the price of one chick. Have children make a dozen pom-pom chicks. Get two egg cartons. Label one "eggs to hatch" and the other one "chicks ready to give." Place each of the twelve chicks in reclosable Easter eggs and place them in the "eggs to hatch" carton. As enough money is raised to buy a chick, let children open up an egg and place the "hatched" chick into the other egg carton. Encourage them to keep raising money until all the eggs are hatched.

• **Read 1 John 3:17.** Talk about how helping others is more important than keeping and spending money on ourselves. Have children raise money to purchase school supplies for children who can't afford them at the beginning of the school year. (Link up with an elementary school in your community to set this up before you start.) Then have children purchase the school supplies needed, using lists provided by the school.

• **Take children to a bakery to purchase cookies to take to a child-care center or your church's pre-school room. Have children serve the cookies to the children.**

Ideas for 10- to 12-Year-olds

• **In the spring, shop for flowers to give to parents with infants and toddlers.** Often parents have little time to shop for items that aren't necessities, and people enjoy receiving flowers in the spring that they can replant and grow.

• **Do a major fund-raiser to raise money for low-income children to go shopping for new shoes.** Partner with a discount store to be a partial sponsor for this fund-raiser and find a social service agency in your community who can identify children who could use this shopping trip. As a group, raise money and work with the store to find a date and time for the children to shop. Have children on hand to assist with this shopping day.

• **Ask someone to read aloud Luke 9:13.** Have children discuss what Jesus calls us to do and the excuses we make. Then have children read verses 14-17 and talk about what happens when we serve despite having doubts. As a group, raise money and shop for stamps. Many people who live on fixed incomes would welcome receiving a gift of stamps because people often need stamps but rarely receive them as gifts.

Helpful organizations

For the address, phone number, and web site of these organizations, see the Mission and Service Index starting on page 119.

• **Heifer Project International**—Buy a gift animal or tree seedling to help families around the world become self-reliant.

• **Operation Christmas Child**—Help children who are in need through this program of the Samaritan's Purse.

· Support ·

One of the best biblical role models of support is the woman named Ruth, who stayed with her mother-in-law, Naomi, after Ruth's husband died. She stayed and worked in the fields of Boaz, even though it would have probably been easier for her to go back to her own country.

Supporting someone is about putting her or his needs first and helping in ways that benefit the person more than they benefit us. Children can participate in large-scale service projects that support others and they can also create their own ways of showing support.

Ideas for 3- to 5-Year-olds

- **Talk about Mark 12:29-31 and how God wants us to love God and love our neighbors.** One way that preschoolers can show their support to other people is by being greeters for a church play, concert, or program. Preschoolers can welcome people and give them a program before people take a seat.
- **Contact your local parks and recreation office to find a short, easy-to-walk trail where preschoolers can walk and clean up the litter along the path.** Talk about the importance of supporting the park trails so that people can enjoy using them.
- **Each week, have a different child be in charge of helping the teacher pass out papers to children in the class.** Talk about how this form of support can benefit not only the teacher but also the children in the class.

Ideas for 6- to 9-Year-olds

- **Have children volunteer to fold the flag at the end of the day for your community's city hall or your elementary school.** (Or find other places that fly flags during the day.) Children can learn how to work together to fold a flag properly, and they often take great pride in doing this type of service.
- **Share the story of 1 Kings 17:1-16, where the widow didn't think she had anything to share or any way to support Elijah.** Explain that children always have ways to support and serve others. For example, children can do this by creating a church suggestion box for children. Once children have placed the suggestion box in a prominent place for children, they can visit each classroom to talk about the box and its purpose. Children can explain that each child has good ideas on how to make church a better place for children and that they want children to share their ideas. Have children check the box each week. Talk about the suggestions and act on them.

• **Create a lost-and-found box for community centers, day-care centers, schools, and other places that need these boxes during the winter months.** Some elementary schools say they collect up to two thousand lost-and-found items during the winter, and they often don't have a place to put these things.

Ideas for 10- to 12-Year-olds

• **Answer phones and assist with simple administrative tasks during a child-care center's lunch hour.** Often people who work for child-care centers do not get breaks due to staff shortages and the constant activity that requires them to handle situations from room to room.

• **Host a senior prom dance at your church.** Have the children organize and publicize this event, encouraging people over the age of sixty to dress up and come to the dance. Talk with people from this age group to find out the music they like to dance to and what refreshments they would most enjoy. As a group, host the event and encourage children to ask some of the seniors to dance.

• **Study Philippians 2:12-18.** Talk about how to support other people with the advice from this scripture passage. As a group, volunteer to wash dishes for a church dinner or luncheon. As you do this together, talk about the different feelings children have about doing this act of service and what they learned from the Philippians 2 passage.

Helpful organizations

For the address, phone number, and web site of these organizations, see the Mission and Service Index starting on page 119.

• **Bread for the World**—This organization helps feed the hungry and advocates for more equitable legislation for people from all socioeconomic groups.

• **Project Concern International**—This organization provides free medical care for children throughout the world.

· Understand ·

Creating a sense of understanding and empathy helps children become more invested in service projects. Understanding others and their situations is what Isaiah 35:3 is all about: "Give strength to hands that are tired and to knees that tremble with weakness" (TEV).

Giving children hands-on situations that allow them to interact with others and experience the life that others have is how we can promote a sense of understanding. Too often, however, we attempt to shield or protect children from the truth. Yet children often do well in situations we're unsure of. They often can be the shining lights to people who are struggling with difficulties and darkness.

Ideas for 3- to 5-Year-olds

● **Teach preschoolers this part of 2 Corinthians 13:11:** "live in peace" (TEV). Talk about how serving others is a way we can bring peace. Have preschoolers participate in a community parade. Preschoolers can sit on a float or be pulled in wagons as they throw candy or other small favors into the crowd. Talk about how we shower other people with peace and joy by doing our part.

● **Put preschoolers in charge of turning off all the lights in the church after a religious service or church program.** Children can go in and out of all the classrooms and other rooms to extinguish the lights. Mention that each week someone has to turn off all the lights and that the preschoolers are serving by doing the job this week.

● **Give preschoolers first-hand experiences of what it's like to have a certain kind of disability.** Cover the lenses of an old pair of eyeglasses with Vaseline and have children take turns wearing them to see what it's like to have poor eyesight. Wrap children's hands shut with long bandages so they can experience what it's like to not be able to use their hands. Have children spend part of the hour sitting on the floor, not using their legs so they know what it's like to not have the use of their legs. Talk about these experiences. Then do a service project to help one of these groups of people, such as making an audiotape of songs for people who cannot see.

Ideas for 6- to 9-Year-olds

● **Have children arrange for a free blood-pressure screening at your church that's open to congregational members and people who live in your community.** Link up with a community clinic to get volunteers and have children learn about blood pressure before the event. On the day of the event, children can distribute written materials and assist others with the screening.

● **Discuss Psalm 133.** Encourage children to memorize the first verse: "How wonderful it is, how pleasant, for God's people to live together in harmony!" (TEV). Contact your local Muscular Dystrophy Association (MDA) to learn more about the disease and to find out how children can help children with muscular dystrophy. (Many MDA chapters have parties for kids with muscular dystrophy that they need volunteer help for.)

● **Have children collect coins to place into a jar over a period of time.** Talk about the important role everyone has in giving money and also in figuring out where the money could go to help others. Once you've stopped collecting the coins, have a congregation-wide service project where people guess how much money you collected in the jar. On entry blanks, have people fill out their name, address, phone number, their guess, and where they think the money should go. Once they have all cast their votes, count the change as a group. Then find the winner. Give the winner a cupcake (or some other token of recognition) and publish the winning number, person, and charity where the money will go. After you give the money to the designated charity, have children meet with the person who suggested the charity to find out why the person picked that organization.

Ideas for 10- to 12-Year-olds

● **Ask someone who knows sign language to teach children how to sign and how to communicate simple, well-known phrases,**

Teaching Kids to Care & Share

such as "Hi," "How are you?" "I'm fine," and "Bye." Then have children interact with children in your church and community who are hearing-impaired and know sign language.

● **Contact bakers, grocery stores, and restaurants in your community to see if your group can collect any unused food that would otherwise be thrown away.** Take to a community shelter or soup kitchen one day.

● **As a group, study 1 Peter 5:1-4.** Talk about what it means to have a real desire to serve. Contact a local grocery store or food co-op where customers have to carry their groceries to the car. Explain that one afternoon your group would like to offer the service of loading groceries into the cars of people who drive up to the entrance. Create numbered tickets to give to interested customers and label each of their bags with that number so that the bags are placed in the correct car.

Helpful organizations

For the address, phone number, and web site of these organizations, see the Mission and Service Index starting on page 119.

● **Angelcare**—This organization serves children who live in poverty throughout the world.

● **Center for Victims of Torture**—Children can provide healing and hope to people who have survived extreme cruelty and torture.

▪ Visit ▪

Serving others through visitation is one of the hallmarks of mission. "Then the King will say to the people on his right, 'Come, you that are blessed by my Father! Come and possess the kingdom which has been prepared for you ever since the creation of the world. I was hungry and you fed me, thirsty and you gave me a drink; I was a stranger and you received me in your homes, naked and you clothed me; I was sick and you took care of me, in prison and you visited me'" (Matthew 25:34-36 TEV).

Children can visit infants in the nursery, toddlers who are playing outside, or a senior sewing circle and not even have to leave the church building. Children also can visit people in their homes and those in the hospital and nursing home. By visiting others, children can learn about how service is more than just doing; it's also about being there.

Ideas for 3- to 5-Year-olds

● **As a group visit your community's sewage plant or garbage dump.** Have children take a token of thanks to give to those who work there.

● **Have preschoolers make a pastoral call—to your pastor.** Even pastors need care, and they often don't have visitors who come with the intention of just visiting them. Preschoolers will think it's so great to go to the pastor's house or pastor's office.

● **Talk about Acts 2:5-11 and how we have a lot in common with people who seem different from us.** Have preschoolers visit a rehabilitation center for people with disabilities or the physical therapy room of a hospital. (Set up an appointment with these places first.) Encourage children to talk and sing songs to meet people there since doing physical therapy and rehabilitation is hard work. Afterward talk about how in Acts all the people thought they were so different from one another, yet they were not, and how people in rehabilitation centers are a lot like us.

Ideas for 6- to 9-Year-olds

- **Read aloud 1 Corinthians 13.** Talk about how we are to love people—every single day. As a group visit a hospice or hospital ward where people are terminally ill. Explain that even though these people are dying, they are still living at the time of your visit. Have children read stories to the people and talk with them.

- **Have children learn about how people can visit through the mail or the Internet.** Adopt a specific military unit stationed overseas. Have children draw pictures or write letters and send them through postal mail or e-mail. During the holidays, children can send small gifts.

- **Create an Easter egg hunt for hospitalized children.** Your children can hide eggs on the bed under the covers and in the folds of the sheets. Or they can hide eggs around the room that can be seen by a child who is bedridden. Ask the child to point to the eggs while a visiting child retrieves them.

Ideas for 10- to 12-Year-olds

- **Study Matthew 20:26-28.** Have children meet with a group of senior citizens (either in your congregation or at a senior center) and plan a joint garden together. Throughout the summer, periodically visit to work together on weeding, replanting, and harvesting the vegetables.

- **Offer to put up and decorate Christmas trees for members of your congregation who are homebound or recovering from an illness or surgery.**

- **Have children play board games with residents at a nursing home.**

Helpful organizations

For the address, phone number, and web site of these organizations, see the Mission and Service Index starting on page 119.

- **Shriners Hospitals for Children**—This network of hospitals offers free medical care to children in need.

- **Sister Cities International**—Support another city by working with your community to become a sister city through this organization. Your church could find a sister church this way.

• Walk/Run •

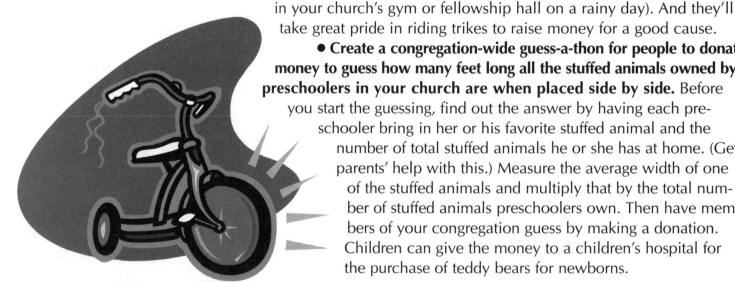

Walk-a-thons and races are popular ways to serve others by gathering pledges and then doing some type of physical activity. Many people enjoy these types of service projects since those raising the money have to not only ask for the money but then earn it. And there's also satisfaction in knowing that you're raising money for every mile you walk.

Second John 4-6 calls us to live in truth and love. By raising money through creative walk-a-thons, children can be messengers of truth, love—and hope.

Ideas for 3- to 5-Year-olds

• **Create opportunities for preschoolers to participate with their families.** Create stroller-a-thons, wagon-a-thons, and walk-a-thons for families with young children. You can even have children put streamers on strollers or wagons to make the service fund-raiser look festive.

• **Talk about Hebrews 12:1 and how we should run for run-a-thons, walk for walk-a-thons, and ride tricycles for trike-a-thons!** Preschoolers will enjoy having a trike-a-thon on your church parking lot (or in your church's gym or fellowship hall on a rainy day). And they'll take great pride in riding trikes to raise money for a good cause.

• **Create a congregation-wide guess-a-thon for people to donate money to guess how many feet long all the stuffed animals owned by preschoolers in your church are when placed side by side.** Before you start the guessing, find out the answer by having each preschooler bring in her or his favorite stuffed animal and the number of total stuffed animals he or she has at home. (Get parents' help with this.) Measure the average width of one of the stuffed animals and multiply that by the total number of stuffed animals preschoolers own. Then have members of your congregation guess by making a donation. Children can give the money to a children's hospital for the purchase of teddy bears for newborns.

Ideas for 6- to 9-Year-olds

• **Have children read aloud and learn Isaiah 40:31.** Talk about how God helps us not get tired when we're serving others. Create a service project where children raise money through a bowl-a-thon. Use plastic juice or soda bottles for pins and a plastic ball. Children can get pledges for the number of pins knocked over.

● **Create a fund-raiser that accentuates what your children do well and are highly interested in.** For example, some children at this age would enjoy a joke-a-thon. Others would do great with a talk-a-thon. Sing-a-thons work well with some groups, as do hopscotch-a-thons with other groups.

● **Have a month-long attendance-a-thon (which not only raises money but also encourages children to boost their Sunday school attendance).** Have classes compete with each other, keeping track of the total number of children present in their class each week. Then have classes total up their attendance at the end of a four-week period. Children can collect pledges based on the classroom totals. Figure out a way to give an award to the class with the highest attendance percentage. Then celebrate on an even grander scale by adding up the total of all the classes together. Thank the congregation for their donations by reporting the total amount collected and the attendance rate. Consider repeating this project each year, challenging attendees and givers to top the numbers achieved the previous year.

Ideas for 10- to 12-Year-olds

● **Have a subject-a-thon, such as a math-a-thon or an English-a-thon, that not only raises money but also challenges children academically.** Work with a teacher to develop math or English workbooks with problems for children to do. Children can raise money by the number of problems they solve correctly.

● **Read aloud 1 Corinthians 9:24-26.** Talk about the stamina needed to do a pledge fund-raiser. Then have a jump-rope-a-thon or a skateboard-a-thon or a bike-a-thon, depending on what children choose. Make sure they choose something they enjoy that also will really challenge them.

● **Have a group bake-a-thon where children bake cookies, cookie bars, and/or cupcakes to raise money for charity.** Some groups raise money by collecting pledges on the number of items baked. Others have a bake sale and raise money by what they sell.

Helpful organizations

For the address, phone number, and web site of these organizations, see the Mission and Service Index starting on page 119.

● **American Diabetes Association**—This organization sponsors its own bike-a-thons to raise money for diabetes research.

● **March of Dimes**—Through its WalkAmerica program, this group has an annual walk-a-thon to raise money for research into how to prevent birth defects and infant mortality.

▪ Welcome ▪

It's easy in our mobile society for people to feel isolated and alone. Making your congregation and community a welcoming place is essential for developing goodwill and relationships. Jesus said in Mark 9:37, "Whoever welcomes in my name one of these children, welcomes me; and whoever welcomes me, welcomes not only me but also the one who sent me" (TEV). By creating mission and service projects that encourage children to welcome others, children become sensitive to others' feelings and learn to reach out to those who are new or alone. And they'll also be doing what Christ said: welcoming God into their midst by welcoming others.

Ideas for 3- to 5-Year-olds

• **Recruit families with young children to hand out bulletins for worship services.** Even preschoolers can hand out bulletins, welcome people, or just hang out and greet people with their parents.

• **Use Matthew 19:13-15 as a way of making your classroom a welcoming place.** Say, "Jesus said, 'Let the children come to me.' That means everybody. Everybody is welcome." Whenever a new child visits, play "I Like." Children sit in a circle, and each child says her or his name and then one thing he or she likes, such as "Susan, and I like ice cream" or "Carlos, and I like dinosaurs." After you finish playing the game, have all the children (except for the visitor) say the new child's name and "We like you!"

• **When a visitor attends a second time, take two Polaroid photos of the group.** Write the names of all the children in the border near their faces. If you have a large class write the names on a separate piece of paper. Give one photo to the visitor and hang the other one on a bulletin board. This helps the visitor feel included and also gives the visitor something tangible to take home and talk about.

Ideas for 6- to 9-Year-olds

• **When a new baby comes to your congregation (through birth or adoption), have children make the baby "welcome pictures."** As a group present them to the parents at a time when the children can meet and greet the new baby.

• **Visit a homebound church member as a group.** Take cookies that the group baked. Have the children sing the person a song. Have each child introduce her- or himself and say two things he or she likes to do. Do things that help the person feel welcome and connected—even though he or she doesn't get out much.

• **Tie Philemon verse 17 into playing the "Welcome Game"**

when visitors come to your class. Say, "Paul encouraged his friend Philemon to welcome Onesimus just like Philemon would welcome Paul. Although Philemon most likely didn't want to see Onesimus again because he was mad at him, Paul said it was good to make Onesimus feel welcome—just like we should help everyone feel welcome." Then play the game by asking children to stand in a circle. Have children take turns jumping into the middle of the circle and saying, "Hi, Kelly (the name of the visitor). I'm Cedric (the child's name)" before jumping back. Have the visitor start the game by introducing her- or himself by saying, "Hi, everybody. I'm Kelly (the visitor's name)."

Ideas for 10- to 12-Year-olds

- **Create a church welcome wagon for new members.** When new members are presented to your congregation, have children wheel out a wagon holding a small welcome gift for each new member, such as a potted plant.
- **As a group, study 3 John verses 9-15, discussing which groups of people your church seems not welcoming towards and why.** In addition, talk about which groups are welcomed—and how they are welcomed. Then analyze your church to see how welcoming it is for: people in wheelchairs, the sick, other ethnic groups, people who are hearing-impaired or sightless, elderly people, the young, and so on. Choose one small thing you can do to become a more welcoming church, such as working with the church staff to invite children to come forward and sit on the floor to see baptisms or to help carpenters build a wooden wheelchair ramp.
- **During congregational mission or service projects, plan games to play with the children of those who are being served.** For example, sometimes children of the family who are having a house painted often feel pushed aside because the focus is on the painting and their parents. Playing games with the children makes them feel welcome and included.
- **Have children take turns being the "welcoming greeter" whenever your group meets or has a class.** This person welcomes visitors and new people by sitting with them, giving them a tour of the room, and helping visitors feel comfortable by talking with them and playing with them. Having children take turns gives each child the opportunity to build skills and avoids having only the children with strong social skills develop them further while leaving those who are still learning without opportunities to practice.

Helpful organizations

For the address, phone number, and web site of these organizations, see the Mission and Service Index starting on page 119.

- **The Carter Center**—This organization, started by former president Jimmy Carter, seeks to make the world a more welcoming place for people who live in difficult and life-threatening circumstances.
- **Welcome Wagon**—Many communities have this organization that welcomes new residents when they move in.

• Write/Draw •

In biblical days, one of the ways people kept in contact and sent warm greetings to one another was through letters. Many of the New Testament books are letters. These letters encourage, support, and challenge people to live in more meaningful, giving ways.

Learning to write is a long process for children, with many learning to write at different ages. Yet children can communicate through the use of paper whether they can write words or draw pictures. Writing and drawing are ways that children can serve others.

Ideas for 3- to 5-Year-olds

• **Talk about Galatians 6:11 and how the writer is so proud of what he can do with his own hand!** Have children dip their hands in finger paint and make a hand print on a piece of 8½-by-11-inch paper. On each paper write one word of service, such as *help, give, care, visit, repair,* and *clean,* and make a display of what children can do with their own two hands.

• **Have preschoolers draw happy face pictures to give to toddlers in your church, children in the hospital, or to members who are sick.**

• **Make a "We Love You" banner for a nursing home or residential care facility.** Have an adult write the words and have children paint, color, use stamp pads, and add stickers to decorate the banner.

Ideas for 6- to 9-Year-olds

• **Draw pictures for your church choir, handbell group, or other musical group in your congregation to show your support and thanks for the music they give.** Encourage children to draw pictures of music. (Play music while they're drawing to get them inspired.) Make a separate picture for the choir director, organist, and accompanist.

• **Read aloud Deuteronomy 11:18-21 to the children.** Talk about how people would write important messages and hang them on their doorposts. Have each child decorate a piece of 8½-by-11-inch paper with light colors or watercolor paints. Then have them write their names over the decoration with black marker. Hang these around the doorway to your classroom. Above the door, label your creation "Those Who Serve." Discuss the important role each person has in service and mission.

• **Draw happy messages and pictures with chalk on sidewalks and driveways on days new parents are to arrive home from the hospital or adoption agency with their new family member.**

Ideas for 10- to 12-Year-olds

● **Read Jude 3.** Ask children to look at the emotion behind the words about writing. Talk about the different feelings children have about writing and drawing. Help them identify at least one area that interests them. Explore writing letters, drawing pictures, painting, writing word or cross-word puzzles, drawing with chalk on the sidewalk, drawing hang-man and tic-tac-toe puzzles, cartooning, writing jokes, doodling, and so on. Figure out ways to tap children's passions for service projects.

● **Encourage children to write letters to the editor of your community newspaper when they see something they really like or are concerned about.** Talk about voicing an opinion as a first step in a service project and emphasize that it's also important to do something about that opinion.

● **Have children draw, paint, and do art projects to sell to raise funds for a cause they deem important.** Adults often enjoy supporting a good cause and being able to purchase children's art. This empowers children too.

● **Have your group create a quarterly children's church newsletter that includes articles about children, news about children's service projects, and drawings that children have made.**

Helpful organizations

For the address, phone number, and web site of these organizations, see the Mission and Service Index starting on page 119.

● **Children's Art Foundation**—To encourage children to develop their potential in art and literacy, this organization works with individuals, schools, libraries, and other child-based organizations.

● **Sadako Peace Project for Children**—This organization links children who want to be pen pals with other children who are interested in world peace.

Part 3

Handouts for Mission & Service

The pages in this section are designed to support your work. They're reproducible handouts that you have permission to photocopy for local church and educational uses only. All together, you'll find eleven ready-to-use handouts, six for adults to use and five for children to use.

The first six reproducible handouts give adults the extra support they need in creating and executing service and mission projects. Photocopy "Service at Home" and distribute copies to the parents and guardians of children while encouraging them to engage their children in acts at service at home. Use the "Choosing Service and Mission Projects" and the "Service and Mission Project Planning Sheet" in setting up projects. Copy the "Service and Mission Project Consent Form" to get permission from parents for their children to engage in acts of service, particularly if you are taking children off-site. Use the "Evaluating the Success of Your Service or Mission Project" form to help you assess a project after it has been completed. The "Service Project Certificate of Achievement" is a form to photocopy and fill out to give to each child after the completion of a service project. Make these certificates look official by adding gold seals to them. A certificate is a tangible reminder to children of the work they've done.

The next five reproducible handouts are for children to use. They include puzzles, a Bible study, and worksheets that emphasize the importance of mission and service. Use the handouts that best fit the age of the children you work with. Some handouts will work with all ages, others are more applicable to older children.

• Service at Home •

Children can serve in many ways at home with their families. Here are some ideas for children of different ages:

Ideas for All Children

- Have a designated service time in your family when everyone pitches in and shares the load of chores.
- Create shared family experiences. It's easier for children to clean their rooms when everyone works together.
- Give children a voice in how to do chores and service projects.
- Break large tasks (such as cleaning a bedroom) into smaller tasks, such as picking up the floor, putting clothes in the laundry chute or basket, making the bed, and so on.
- Make service and helping times fun.
- Volunteer together as a family to do a service or mission project.

Ideas for 3- to 5-Year-olds

- Put a napkin at each place setting.
- Stir the cookie dough batter.
- Pick one to three favorite toys to put away when a friend comes to play and share the rest of the toys.
- Drop off canned goods for a food drive.
- Help choose a gift for a family member.
- Save energy by turning off lights and the television.
- Put bathtub toys in a bucket after the bath.
- Pick up sticks in the grass.
- Wipe up spills on the floor.
- Get diapers for a younger sibling.
- Tear lettuce or bread chicken cutlets.
- Carry plates and dirty silverware to the sink or dishwasher after a meal.

Ideas for 6- to 9-Year-olds

- Pick up toys and put them away after using them.
- Put dirty laundry in laundry basket or clothes chute.
- Wipe dishes after someone older washes them.
- Vacuum.
- Pick up clothes from the laundry and put them away.
- Dust furniture.
- Straighten up the bed.
- Take out trash.
- Empty the dishwasher.
- Mix juice, lemonade, or Kool-Aid.
- Check items off a shopping list during a family shopping trip.
- Plant seeds in a garden.

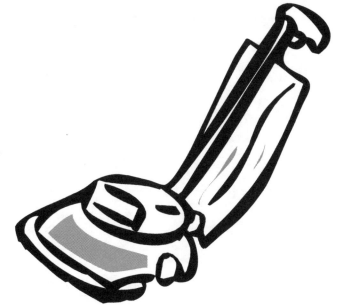

Ideas for 10- to 12-Year-olds

- Collect used clothing to give away.
- Bake cookies for a sick family member, friend, or neighbor.
- Write a letter to a grandparent or other family member.
- Set the table.
- Make one's own bag lunch for school.
- Clean the bedroom.
- Rake the leaves.
- Unpack groceries.
- Set food on the table.
- Change bed linens.
- Make and send birthday cards.
- Clip coupons out of the Sunday paper for items the family frequently buys.

▪ Choosing Service ▪ and Mission Projects

Before you actually commit to doing a service project, use this evaluation form to see if the project you're interested in doing with children fits the seven keys of meaningful mission and service.

Seven keys of service and mission

	Yes	No
Key #1: Is the project concrete?	❑	❑
Key #2: Are you working with an existing network?	❑	❑
Key #3: Does the project empower children?	❑	❑
Key #4: Do you plan to debrief the children about the experience afterward?	❑	❑
Key #5: Have you lined up all the important resources you need?	❑	❑
Key #6: Does the project fit with your church's mission?	❑	❑
Key #7: Is the project fun for children?	❑	❑

Other things to consider

	Yes	No
● Does the project promote relationship building between children?	❑	❑
● Do you have a way to keep parents and church members informed?	❑	❑
● Will the project allow children to interact with a different group of people from your church (such as the youth group or a senior group)?	❑	❑
● Will the project engage families in some way?	❑	❑
● Have you identified what you want children to learn from this service project?	❑	❑
● Are you satisfied with the project you've chosen?	❑	❑

• Evaluating the Success of • Your Service or Mission Project

Once you complete a service or mission project, take time to reflect and assess what happened. Evaluating your project will provide helpful information for the next project.

Service or mission project title: _____

Date of project (including the day of the week): _____

Project leader or coordinator: _____

Number of children who participated: _____

The age of children who participated: _____

What did you hope children would gain through participating in this service or mission project?

_____

How were your hopes met or unmet? _____

_____

What surprised you most about the project experience?

_____

What frustrated or disappointed you most about the project experience?

_____

What would you change the next time you did a project like this with children?

_____

What was most successful about the project?

_____

Questions to Ask Children Who Participated

Orally ask children individually about their experience to get their feedback.

• What did you like best about this project?

• What did you like least about this project?

• Overall did you like doing this project? Why or why not?

• Would you do this project again? Why or why not?

• Would you like to do another project? If so, what kind? If not, why not?

▪ Service and Mission Project ▪ Planning Sheet

The service project: _____

Date and time of the service project: _____

Purpose of the project: _____

_____

Who the project will serve: _____

How the service project benefits the children doing the project: _____

_____

Anticipated outcomes of the service project: _____

_____

If you're raising money, what percentage of the proceeds will be donated to which causes:

_____%   Cause to receive the money: _____

_____%   Cause to receive the money: _____

_____%   Cause to receive the money: _____

_____%   Cause to receive the money: _____

Approval for the service project has been granted by:

❑ Children   ❑ Parents   ❑ Adults involved   ❑ The governing body of your church

Supplies needed for the service project:

_____

_____

_____

_____

_____

_____

_____

Adult helpers for the service project (their names and phone numbers):

_____

_____

_____

_____

Consent forms sent to and received back from the parents and guardians of these children:

_____

_____

_____

_____

_____

Is the service project on your church's calendar?   ❑ Yes   ❑ No

What refreshments are needed:

_____

_____

_____

_____

_____

The evaluation you plan to do afterward:

_____

_____

_____

▪ Service and Mission Project ▪ Consent Form

Today's date: _____

TO: The parent(s) or guardian(s) of: _____

We will be doing a service project that we would like your child to participate in.
Before your child can do so, however, we must receive your written consent.
Please read and sign the attached form by _____ .

Here are details about the service project: _____

What we will be doing: _____

The date we will be doing it: _____

The times of the project: _____

Anything your child needs for participation: _____

We appreciate your and your child's interest in doing this service project. If you have any questions or concerns, please feel free to contact me.

My name: _____ .

My phone number: _____ .

- -

Consent Form

I give permission for _____ to participate

in the service project on _____ (date of project).

_____
Printed name of parent or guardian

_____
Signature of parent or guardian

_____
Today's date

SERVICE PROJECT
Certificate of Achievement

Awarded to

_____

In recognition of outstanding participation

in _____

"Then the King will say to the people on his right, 'Come, you that are blessed by my Father! Come and possess the kingdom which has been prepared for you ever since the creation of the world. I was hungry and you fed me, thirsty and you gave me a drink; I was a stranger and you received me in your homes, naked and you clothed me; I was sick and you took care of me, in prison and you visited me. . . . Whenever you did this for one of the least important of these followers of mine, you did it for me!' "
(Matthew 25:34-36, 40 TEV)

_____
(Signature)

· Helping God by ·
Helping Others

Color in all the spaces that have an *A, C,* or *T* and see what the word spells. For an even bigger challenge, count the number of times you can find the words *Love* and *Act* in the puzzle.

L	L	O	V	E	L	O	V	E	L	O	V	E	L	O	V	E	L	O	V	E	L	O
O	A	C	T	V	A	C	T	V	A	C	T	A	O	A	E	V	A	E	A	C	T	L
V	C	L	V	O	C	L	V	O	C	L	O	C	V	C	V	O	C	V	C	V	E	O
E	T	C	A	L	T	A	E	L	A	C	T	T	E	T	O	L	T	O	T	A	L	V
L	O	V	C	O	C	L	V	O	C	V	C	O	V	A	L	E	A	L	C	L	O	E
O	A	C	T	V	A	C	T	V	T	E	L	T	O	V	C	T	O	V	A	C	T	L
V	L	O	V	E	L	O	V	E	L	O	V	E	L	O	V	E	L	O	V	E	L	O

Teaching Kids to Care & Share

Helping God by Helping Others

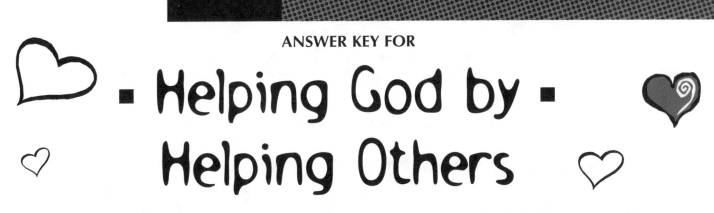

Color in all the spaces that have an *A, C,* or *T* and see what the word spells. For an even bigger challenge, count the number of times you can find the words *Love* and *Act* in the puzzle.

The missing word is *SERVE.*
Love appears 21 times.
Act appears 19 times.

▪ Helping Heroes ▪

Many children come up with creative ways to serve others. Read the short stories about real-life helping heroes. Then write your idea on how to serve others in the empty space on the next page.

A playground should be a fun place for all children, including children in wheelchairs, said 12-year-old Caroline Merrey. So she spent two years researching, planning, designing, and raising funds to build a new playground in her Baltimore neighborhood. "I have learned that you must be patient and persistent, and you must convince people that your cause is worthwhile," Caroline says. "It's a wonderful feeling to finally see children playing on our new playground."
—*The Lutheran,* March 1998, p. 21

When David Levitt of Largo, Florida, was 11 years old, he noticed the large amount of food that was thrown away and wasted at the school cafeteria. David asked the school board if he could gather up the leftover food and donate it to hungry people. The school board said yes, and David began an organization called Food for Thought, which is still in existence.
—Ziv Tzedakah Fund newsletter, 1 April 1999, p. 3

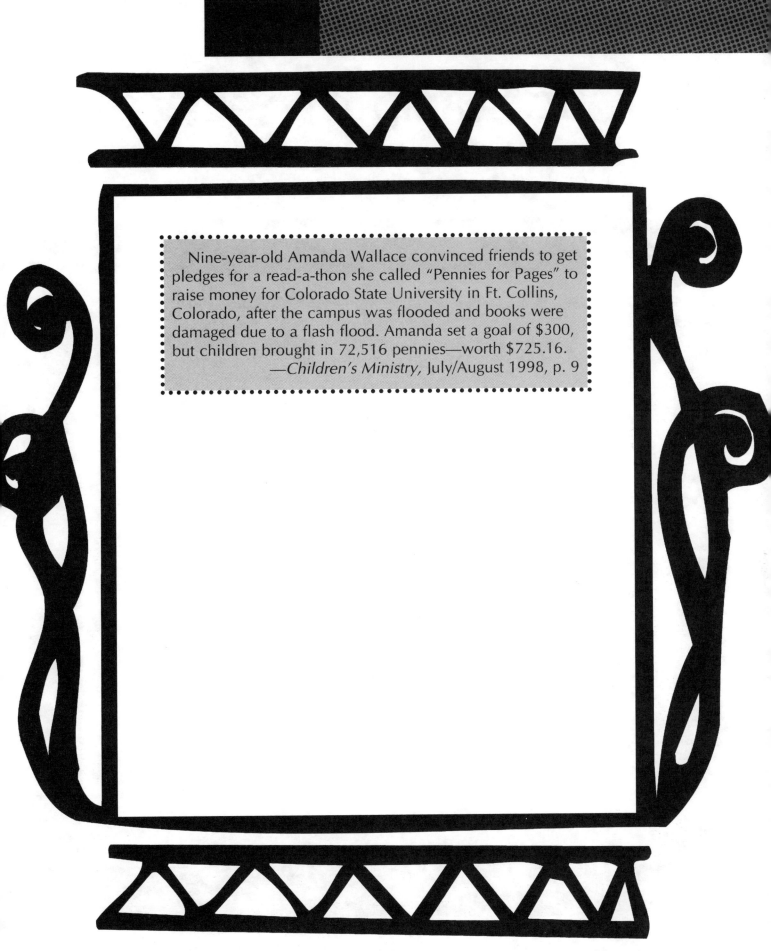

Nine-year-old Amanda Wallace convinced friends to get pledges for a read-a-thon she called "Pennies for Pages" to raise money for Colorado State University in Ft. Collins, Colorado, after the campus was flooded and books were damaged due to a flash flood. Amanda set a goal of $300, but children brought in 72,516 pennies—worth $725.16.
—*Children's Ministry,* July/August 1998, p. 9

▪ Your Stamp of Service ▪

Design a postage stamp that best describes your view of service and mission. Be creative. What image best represents your view? How much money do you think the postage stamp should sell for?

Teaching Kids to Care & Share

▪ Putting the Pieces Together ▪

On the puzzle below, each puzzle piece has a scripture passage. Look up the scripture and write on the puzzle piece what that scripture says about service or mission.

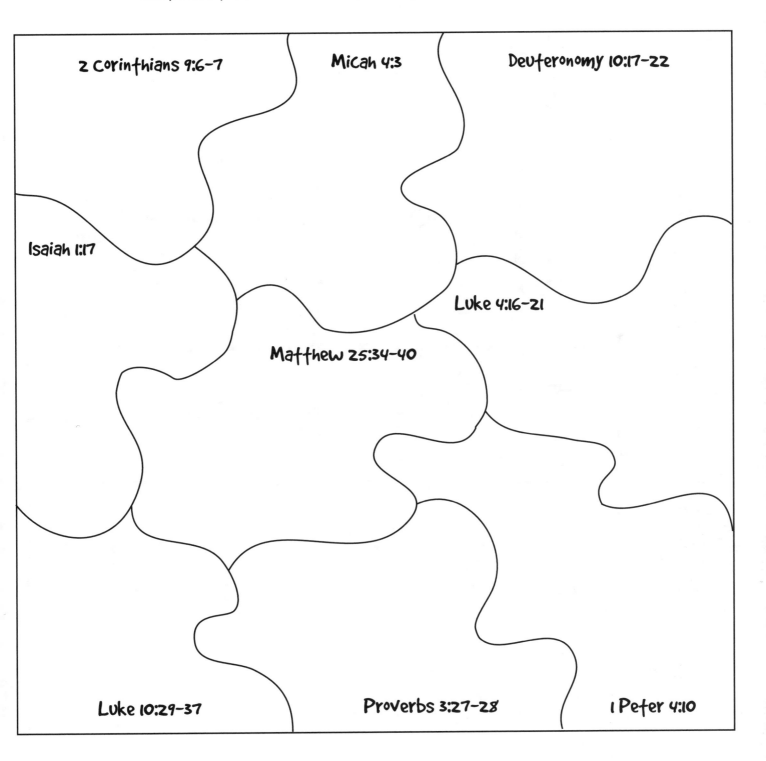

2 Corinthians 9:6-7

Micah 4:3

Deuteronomy 10:17-22

Isaiah 1:17

Luke 4:16-21

Matthew 25:34-40

Luke 10:29-37

Proverbs 3:27-28

1 Peter 4:10

■ Brick by Brick, Row by Row ■

Insert the following action words of service into the wall below to show how service is built brick by brick, row by row. Each of the missing words appears horizontally on the brick wall. Only the word SERVICE appears up and down.

3-letter word
ACT

4-letter words
HELP
GIVE
CARE

5-letter words
CLEAN
VISIT

7-letter word
MISSION

• Brick by Brick, Row by Row •

Insert the following action words of service into the wall below to show how service is built brick by brick, row by row. Each of the missing words appears horizontally on the brick wall. Only the word *SERVICE* appears up and down.

3-letter word	4-letter words	5-letter words	7-letter word
ACT	HELP	CLEAN	MISSION
	GIVE	VISIT	
	CARE		

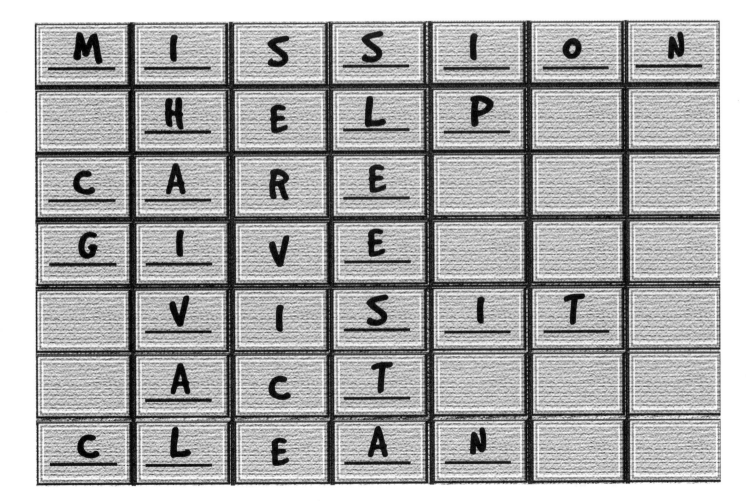

Notes

Part 1: The Beginnings of Mission and Service

1. Dorothy Day, quoted in Robert Coles, *The Call of Service: A Witness to Idealism* (Boston: Houghton Mifflin, 1993), xxiii.

2. *Volunteering and Giving,* ed. Virginia A. Hodgkinson et al. (Washington, D.C.: Independent Sector, 1997), 23, 25.

3. Ibid., 23.

4. Ibid., 25.

5. Ann Shoemaker, *Teaching Young Children Through Service* (St. Paul: National Youth Leadership Council, 1999), 6.

6. Louise Bates Ames, Ph.D.; Frances L. Ilg, M.D.; and Sidney M. Baker, M.D., *Your Ten- to Fourteen-Year-Old* (New York: Dell, 1988), 221.

7. Eugene C. Roehlkepartain, Thomas Bright, and Beth Margolis-Rupp, *An Asset-Builder's Guide to Service-Learning* (Minneapolis: Search Institute, 1999). Chapter 3, titled "Making Service-Learning Work for All Kids," includes many practical suggestions on how to work with children of different ages, how to work with families, how to work with intergenerational groups, how to work with children with disabilities, and how to work with young people who are considered "marginalized" or, as some people call these children, "at risk," "disadvantaged," or "vulnerable."

Part 2: The Actions of Mission and Service

1. Shel Silverstein, *The Giving Tree* (New York: Harper & Row, 1964).

2. Ed Emberley, *Go Away, Big Green Monster!* (Boston: Little, Brown and Co., 1992).

3. For more information, see the month of September in *Chase's Annual Events,* published yearly by Contemporary Books.

4. Faye Wilson-Beach, *Great Mission Ideas for Workers with Children,* rev. ed. (Cincinnati: General Board of Global Ministries Service Center, 1991), 48.

5. Ziv Tzedakah Fund annual newsletter, 1 April 1999, 25.

Scripture Index

Mission & Service Index

Alzheimer's Association
P.O. Box 5675
Chicago, IL 60680
(800) 272-3900
www.alz.org
People suffering from
Alzheimer's disease are sup-
ported through this organization.

■

American Diabetes Association
1660 Duke Street
Alexandria, VA 22314
(800) DIABETES
www.diabetes.org
This organization sponsors its
own bike-a-thons to raise
money for diabetes research.

■

American Red Cross
430 17th Street NW
Washington, DC 20006
(800) 797-8022
www.redcross.org
By providing food, shelter, medical assistance, and other
necessities, this organization
helps those who live in places
that have been hit by disaster.

■

America the Beautiful Fund
1730 K Street, NW, Suite 1002
Washington, DC 20006
(202) 638-1649
This organization offers free seed
packets for planting when you

send $12 to cover the shipping
of the first set of 100 packets.

■

Angelcare
P.O. Box 83220
San Diego, CA 92138-3220
(800) 842-2810
www.childrensaid.org
This organization serves children who live in poverty
throughout the world.

■

**Big Brothers/Big Sisters of
America**
230 North 13th Street
Philadelphia, PA 19107
(215) 567-7000
www.bbbsa.org
In this mentoring program,
adult volunteers are matched
with children and youth to give
them the extra support young
people need.

■

Bread for the World
1100 Wayne Avenue,
Suite 1000
Silver Spring, MD 20910
(800) 82-BREAD
(301) 608-2400
www.bread.org
This organization helps feed the
hungry and advocates for more
equitable legislation for people
of all socioeconomic levels.

The Carter Center
453 Freedom Parkway
Atlanta, GA 30307
(404) 331-3900
www.cartercenter.org
This organization seeks to make
the world a more welcoming
place for people who live under
difficult and life-threatening circumstances.

■

**The Center for Victims of
Torture**
717 East River Road
Minneapolis, MN 55455
(612) 626-1400
Children can provide healing
and hope to people who have
survived extreme cruelty and
torture.

■

Children's Art Foundation
P.O. Box 83
Santa Cruz, CA 95063
(408) 426-5557
www.stonesoup.com
To encourage children to develop their artistic and literacy
potential, this organization
works with individuals, schools,
libraries, and other child-based
organizations. It also publishes
Stone Soup, the magazine by
young writers and artists.

The Children's Rainforest
P.O. Box 936
Lewiston, ME 04243
(207) 784-1069
Help save Costa Rica's rain forest by supporting this organization's Children's Project.

■

Church World Service
28606 Phillips Street
P.O. Box 968
Elkhart, IN 46515
(800) 297-1516
www.churchworldservice.org
A ministry of the National Council of Churches, this organization helps people in more than 80 countries.

■

Common Cents New York Inc.
104 West 88th Street
New York, NY 10024
(212) 579-0579
By accepting donations of pennies, this organization raises money for people who are homeless.

■

Community Partnerships with Youth, Inc.
6319 Constitution Drive
Fort Wayne, IN 46804
(219) 436-4402
www.cpyinc.org
This organization brings young people and adults together to address neighborhood needs.

■

Compassion International
Colorado Springs, CO 80997
(800) 336-7676
www.ci.org
Sponsor a child in need through this organization. Often a classroom of children sponsors one child.

Direct Relief International
27 South La Patera Lane
Santa Barbara, CA 93117
(800) 676-1638
www.directrelief.org
This organization provides medical assistance to people throughout the world who live in areas that are facing emergencies.

■

Disability Rights Education and Defense Fund, Inc.
2212 Sixth Street
Berkeley, CA 94710
(510) 644-2555
Educate others about how to help people live with physical impairments with information from this organization.

■

Federation for Children with Special Needs
1135 Tremont Street
Boston, MA 02120
(617) 236-7210
www.fcsn.org
This organization works with children who have a variety of physical, mental, and emotional impairments.

■

Food for the Hungry
7729 East Greenway Road
Scottsdale, AZ 85260
(800) 2-HUNGER
(602) 998-3100
www.fh.org
Besides providing disaster relief, this organization also provides self-support help for people who are hungry.

■

Food Works
64 Main Street
Montpelier, VT 05602
(802) 223-1515
School and community gardens

provide food for the hungry through this organization.

■

Fresh Air Fund
1040 Avenue of the Americas
New York, NY 10018
(212) 221-0900
www.freshair.org
Advocate for clean air through this organization.

■

Friends of the Earth
1025 Vermont Avenue, NW,
Third Floor
Washington, DC 20005-6303
(202) 783-7400
www.foe.org
This organization provides information on ways to improve the environment.

■

Generations United
440 First Street, NW, Fourth Floor
Washington, DC 20001-2085
(202) 662-4283
www.gu.org
Part of the Child Welfare League, this program promotes intergenerational understanding and interaction.

■

The Giraffe Project
P.O. Box 759
Langley, WA 98260
(360) 221-7989
www. giraffe.org
This organization encourages children and adults to "stick their necks out" to make the world a better place by working on problems such as pollution, hunger, and violence.

■

Goodwill Industries of America Inc.
(800) 664-6577
www.goodwill.org

Look in your local white pages for the Goodwill nearest you. Or contact your local community volunteer organization to find out how to get in touch with this organization.

■

Habitat for Humanity
121 Habitat Street
Americus, GA 31709-3498
(800) 422-4828
http://www.habitat.org
By building and repairing homes throughout the United States and around the world, this organization is doing essential work in providing housing for many people who can't afford it.

■

Heifer Project International
P.O. Box 8106
Little Rock, AR 72203-8106
(800) 422-0755
http://www.heifer.org
Buy a gift animal or tree seedling to help families around the world become self-reliant.

■

The Hole in the Wall Gang Fund
555 Long Wharf Drive
New Haven, CT 06511
(203) 772-0522
http://www.holeinthewallgang.org
This camp caters to children with serious health problems.

■

Kids Care Clubs
P.O. Box 1083
New Canaan, CT 06840
(203) 972-6601
http:www.kidscare.org
Have your children write a letter explaining why they want to help others and this organization will send you information with ideas from other kids. You

also can become a member of this national organization and receive newsletters of ideas.

■

Kids Cheering Kids
P.O. Box 2359
Las Gatos, CA 95031
(888) KIDS-PLAY
www.kidscheeringkids.org
People from ages 5 to 23 work to create a better world for children who have less than they do. They share their time, allowance, and optimism.

■

Kids for a Clean Environment
(Kids F.A.C.E.)
P.O. Box 158254
Nashville, TN 37215
(615) 331-7381
www.kidsface.org
An environmental action club for children, this organization has a newsletter that keeps those interested in environmental issues up to date.

■

Kids for Saving Earth (KSE)
P.O. Box 421118
Minneapolis, MN 55442
(612) 559-1234
This kids' environmental action club produces a newsletter full of ideas.

■

Lutheran Braille Workers, Inc.
13471 California Street
P.O. Box 5000
Yucaipa, CA 92399
(909) 795-8977
users.aol.com/LBWBraille/lbw.htm
This organization provides Braille and large-print Bibles and Christian reading materials to people with visual impairments.

Make-A-Wish Foundation
100 West Clarendon, Suite 2200
Phoenix, AZ 85013-3518
(800) 722-WISH
www.wish.org
This organization grants wishes to children with life-threatening illnesses.

■

March of Dimes
233 Park Avenue South, Third Floor
New York, NY 10003
(888) MODIMES
www.modimes.org
Through its WalkAmerica program, this group has an annual walk-a-thon to raise money for research into how to prevent birth defects and infant mortality.

■

Meals on Wheels
This organization provides meals to people who can no longer cook through volunteers who deliver meals to their door. Look in your local white pages for the Meals on Wheels nearest you. Or contact your local community volunteer organization to find out how to get in touch with this organization.

■

National Arbor Day Foundation
211 North 12th Street
Lincoln, NE 68508
(402) 474-5655
http://www.arborday.org
Emphasizing the importance of trees, this organization offers free seedlings for planting.

■

National Council on the Aging
409 Third Street, SW
Washington, DC 20024
(202) 479-1200
www.ncoa.org

This organization aims to improve the lives of the elderly.

■

National Crime Prevention Council
1700 K Street, NW, Second Floor
Washington, DC 20006-3817
(202) 466-6272
www.weprevent.org
This organization enables people to prevent crime while building safer, more caring communities.

■

National Safe Kids Campaign
1301 Pennsylvania Avenue, NW, Suite 1000
Washington, DC 20004-1707
(202) 662-0600
www.safekids.org
This national campaign advocates that all children be safe from crime and abuse.

■

National Youth Leadership Council
1910 West County Road B
St. Paul, MN 55113
(651) 631-3672
http://www.nylc.org
This organization combines service with learning and offers programs and publications for doing service with children and youth.

■

Natural Guard
142 Howard Avenue
New Haven, CT 06519
(203) 787-0229
This hands-on organization helps children identify and solve their local community's problems.

■

One Plus One
C/O WQED Video

4802 Fifth Avenue
Pittsburgh, PA 15213
(800) 274-1307
A clearinghouse of information, this organization offers print and video materials on the topic of mentoring.

■

Operation Christmas Child
Samaritan's Purse
P.O. Box 3000
Boone, NC 28607
(800) 353-5949
www.samaritan.org
Help children who are in need through this program of the Samaritan's Purse.

■

Oxfam America
26 West Street
Boston, MA 02111
(800) 77-OXFAM
www.oxfamamerica.org
By being creative with its resources, this organization aims to help the world's neediest people work toward a life free from hunger and poverty.

■

Points of Light Foundation
1400 I Street, NW, Suite 800
Washington, DC 20005
(202) 729-8209
www.pointsoflight.org
This national organization has key information on service and mission on a national and local level.

■

Prevent Child Abuse America
200 South Michigan Avenue, 17th Floor
Chicago, IL 60604-2404
(312) 663-3520
www.childabuse.org
An educational clearinghouse, this organization offers information about all the various forms of child abuse.

Prison Fellowship
P.O. Box 17500
Washington, DC 20041-0500
(703) 478-0100
www.prisonfellowship.org
Get in touch with and serve people who are in prison through this organization.

■

Project Concern International
3550 Afton Road
San Diego, CA 92123
(619) 279-9690
www.serve.com/PCI
This organization provides free medical care for children throughout the world.

■

Puppeteers of America
5 Cricklewood Path
Pasadena, CA 91107-1002
www.puppeteers.org
Amateur and professional puppeteers and those interested in puppets receive information and services from this organization, which can also help you contact your local puppetry guild.

■

Reading Is Fundamental
600 Maryland Avenue, SW, Suite 600
Washington, DC 20024-2520
(202) 287-3220
(877) RIF-READ
www.rif.org
Give the gift of books through this organization so that children who are homeless or at risk can learn to read.

■

Recording for the Blind and Dyslexic
20 Roszel Road
Princeton, NJ 08540
(800) 221-4792
http://www.rfbd.org

This organization provides recordings for people with visual impairments.

■

Sadako Peace Project for Children
P.O. Box 1253
Issaquah, WA 98027-1253
(425) 391-4797
www.sadako.org/SadakoHome.htm
This organization links children who want to be pen pals with other children who are interested in world peace.

■

St. Jude's Ranch for Children
100 St. Jude's Street
P.O. Box 60100
Boulder City, NV 89006-0100
(800) 492-3562
(702) 294-7100
www.stjudesranch.org
Children in this organization recycle used greeting cards that people from across the country send to them in order to make new ones.

■

Save the Children
54 Wilton Road
Westport, CT 06880
(800) 243-5075
This organization sponsors a number of programs to help children who live in poverty throughout the world.

■

Second Harvest
116 South Michigan Avenue, Suite 4
Chicago, IL 60603
(312) 263-2303
www.secondharvest.org
This network of national food banks distributes food to shelters, senior citizen centers, and soup kitchens.

SERVEnet
1101 Fifteenth Street, Suite 200
Washington, DC 20005
(202) 296-2992
www.servenet.org
Find out about volunteer opportunities in your community through this organization.

■

Shriners Hospitals for Children
International Headquarters
2900 Rocky Point Drive
Tampa, FL 33607-1460
(813) 281-0300
http://www.shrinershq.org
This network of hospitals offers free medical care to children in need.

■

Sister Cities International
1300 Pennsylvania Avenue, NW, Suite 250
Washington, DC 20004
(202) 312-1200
www.sister-cities.org
Support another city by working with your community to become a sister city through this organization. Your church could find a sister church this way.

■

Special Olympics International
1325 G Street, NW, Suite 500
Washington, DC 20005
(202) 628-3630
www.specialolympics.org
This organization gives information about the Special Olympic competitions for people with disabilities.

■

Starlight Children's Foundation
5900 Wilshire Boulevard, Suite 2530
Los Angeles, CA 90036
(323) 634-0080
www.starlight.org
Children who are seriously ill

can have their wishes fulfilled through this organization.

■

Sunshine Foundation
2001 Bridge Street
Philadelphia, PA 19124
(215) 535-1413
www.sunshinefoundation.org
This organization promotes hope for children who are seriously ill.

■

Toys for Tots
Marine Corps Base, Quantico
P.O. Box 1947
Quantico, VA 22134
www.toysfortots.org
This organization collects toys to give to children who have little.

■

UNICEF
3 United Nations Plaza
New York, NY 10017
(212) 326-7000
www.unicef.org
The only organization of the United Nations dedicated solely to the welfare of children, UNICEF meets children's basic needs and advocates and works to protect children's rights.

■

The United Methodist Children's Fund for Christian Mission
P.O. Box 845
Nashville, TN 37202-0845
(615) 340-7013
http://www.gbod.org
A joint program of the United Methodist General Board of Discipleship and the General Board of Global Ministries, the organization offers packets for congregations to use with children so that children can learn about and make contributions to a select group of mission projects.

United Way of America

701 North Fairfax Street
Alexandria, VA 22314-2045
(703) 836-7100
www.unitedway.org
The Young America Cares program of the United Way of America has many ideas on how your group can partner with them in volunteer efforts.

■

USA Toy Library Association

2530 Crawford Avenue,
Suite 111
Evanston, IL 60201
(847) 864-3330
www.sjdccd.cc.ca.us/toylibrary
By facilitating the development of toy lending libraries and other programs, this organization promotes the importance of play for children.

■

U.S. National Committee for the World Food Day

2175 K Street, NW
Washington, DC 20437
(202) 653-2404
This organization has projects that children can be involved in for World Food Day.

■

Welcome Wagon

Look in your local white pages for the Welcome Wagon nearest you. Or contact your local community volunteer organization to find out how to get in touch with this organization.

■

YMCA of the USA

101 North Wacker Drive
Chicago, IL 60606
(800) USA-YMCA
(312) 977-0031
www.ymca.net
Recreational, educational, and social programs are offered through this organization.